Relativized Minimality

Linguistic Inquiry Monographs
Samuel Jay Keyser, general editor

Relativized Minimality   Luigi Rizzi

The MIT Press
Cambridge, Massachusetts
London, England

This book was set in Times Roman by the DEKR Corporation. It was printed and bound in the United States of America.

Library of Congress Cataloging-in-Publication Data

Rizzi, Luigi, 1952–
  Relativized minimality / Luigi Rizzi.

   p.   cm. — (Linguistic inquiry monographs; 16)
  Includes bibliographical references.
  ISBN 0-262-18136-3. — ISBN 0-262-68061-0 (pbk.)
  1. Government (Grammar) I. Title. II. Series.
P299.G68R5   1990
415 — dc20   89-49032
                                                            CIP

Contents

Contents

Series Foreword

We are pleased to present this monograph as the sixteenth in the series *Linguistic Inquiry Monographs*. These monographs will present new and original research beyond the scope of the article, and we hope they will benefit our field by bringing to it perspectives that will stimulate further research and insight.

Originally published in limited edition, the *Linguistic Inquiry Monograph* series is now available on a much wider scale. This change is due to the great interest engendered by the series and the needs of a growing readership. The editors wish to thank the readers for their support and welcome suggestions about future directions the series might take.

Samuel Jay Keyser
for the Editorial Board

Foreword

Locality is a pervasive property in natural-language syntax. If there is no upper limit to the length and depth of structural representations, a fundamental core of syntactic processes are bound to apply in local domains. The study of the nature and properties of these domains is the central task of much current work in syntactic theory. There are two conceptually distinct ways of addressing the issue of locality. The first is that certain structural boundaries count as barriers for the process under investigation. Classical Subjacency is a case in point. The second is to assume that the process cannot apply across an intervening element of a designated kind, which could in principle be involved in the process. Various versions of the Specified Subject Condition of the Theory of Binding and of the Minimal Distance Principle of the Theory of Control have this property. Ever since Chomsky 1981, both concepts have been used in distinct characterizations of the fundamental local relation of grammatical theory, the government relation.

This monograph is devoted to exploring the consequences of a particular "intervention" approach to the theory of government. The guiding idea is to maximize the role of intervention, and to correspondingly reduce the role of barriers in the definition of government. The principle to be developed, Relativized Minimality, blocks government of some kind across an element which could bear a government relation of the same kind. Chapter 1 introduces the principle and shows that it permits a unified treatment, under the Empty Category Principle (ECP), of three distinct but intuitively related classes of facts: Huang's (1982) selective violations of *wh* islands, Obenauer's (1984) pseudo-opacity effects, and Ross's (1983) inner islands. Chapter 2 develops a new approach to COMP-trace phenomena through a conjunctive formulation of the ECP, and explores the consequences of conjunctive ECP in various domains. Chapter 3 goes back to the fundamental argument-adjunct asymmetries discussed throughout the book, and proposes a new approach based on a radical simplification of the ECP and a natural constraint on the possible occurrence of referential indices: referential indices are allowed to occur only on elements having referential properties, in a sense to be made precise.

The ideas discussed in the first two chapters were originally presented in a course that I taught jointly with Richard Kayne at MIT in the fall 1986 semester and subsequently refined in a course at the 1987 LSA Summer Linguistic Institute at Stanford (the draft circulated as Rizzi 1987 corresponds to this stage of elaboration), in various courses and presentations at the Séminaire de recherche of the University of Geneva, in a GLOW talk (Budapest, March 1988), and in a talk given at the Second Princeton Workshop on Comparative Grammar (April 1989). The first chapter also draws from previous work on the ECP that I had the opportunity to present and discuss at the Symposium on Formal Syntax and Semantics (University of Texas, Austin, 1985) and at the Workshop on Logical Form (LSA Summer Institute at CUNY, July 1986). The content of the third chapter was originally presented at the University of Geneva in 1987 and was refined in talks at the Meeting of the Linguistic Association of Great Britain (Durham, March 1988) and at the workshop "The Chomskian Turn" (Tel-Aviv and Jerusalem, April 1988; see Rizzi 1988). I am much indebted for helpful comments to the audiences of these events—particularly Maggie Browning and Julia Horvath, discussants of the papers presented at the Princeton and Israel workshops—and to Adriana Belletti, Luigi Burzio, Noam Chomsky, Guglielmo Cinque, Maria Teresa Guasti, Liliane Haegeman, Richard Kayne, Ian Roberts, Dominique Sportiche, Tarald Taraldsen, Sten Vikner, and Eric Wehrli.

Geneva, June 1989

Relativized Minimality

Chapter 1
Opacity Effects on Adjunct Variables

1.1 Introduction

The minimality principle is a partial characterization of the locality conditions on government. The core case to be captured is that a governor cannot govern inside the domain of another governor; i.e., in configuration (1), X cannot govern Y if there is a closer potential governor Z for Y.

(1) . . . X . . . Z . . . Y . . .

The functional correlate of this formal principle is the reduction of ambiguity in government relations: there will be exactly one governor for each governee in the general case. For instance, in a configuration like (2), the verb will not govern the prepositional object *John* because of the intervention of the preposition, a closer potential (and actual) governor.

(2) . . . . [talk [to John]] . . .

Most current definitions implement this core idea in an asymmetric way with respect to the kinds of government. The theory specifies two kinds of government, depending on the nature of the governor: head government (relevant for Case, Binding, and the modules licensing the various types of empty categories) and antecedent government (relevant for the ECP and/or for the definition of chain—see chapter 3). The asymmetry is that an intervening potential head governor blocks both kinds of government, whereas an intervening potential antecedent governor does not have any blocking capacity. That is, if Z is a potential head governor for Y in (1), X can neither head-govern nor antecedent-govern Y, whereas if Z is a potential antecedent governor for Y, both kinds of government are still possible from X. This is, in essence, the effect of the minimality principle of Chomsky (1986b), even though the blocking capacity of an intervening head is indirect in that system, mediated through the notion "barrier".[1] We will call an asymmetric principle of this sort Rigid Minimality.

In this chapter we will explore the consequences of a symmetric approach to minimality. The principle to be introduced, Relativized Minimality, makes the blocking effect of an intervening governor relative to the nature of the government relation involved: in (1), if Z is a potential governor *of some kind* for Y, it will block only government *of the same kind* from X. If Z is a potential head governor, only head government from X will be blocked. If Z is a potential antecedent governor, only antecedent government will be blocked.

Conceptually, this symmetric approach appears to be closer to the intuitive functional correlate of disambiguation, as expressed above. Empirically, the symmetric approach is both more and less restrictive than the asymmetric approach. It is more restrictive because relativized minimality blocks antecedent government from X when Z is a potential antecedent governor, a configuration about which rigid minimality has nothing to say. The symmetric approach is also less restrictive because relativized minimality cannot block antecedent government from X if Z is a potential head governor, whereas rigid minimality does. Within the symmetric approach, head government and antecedent government proceed on parallel tracks and cannot interfere with each other.

The main empirical motivation for relativized minimality has to do with its more restrictive character. It will be argued that this approach permits a unified treatment, under the Empty Category Principle, of three empirical domains which are intuitively very close:

• Huang's (1982) observation that adjuncts cannot be extracted from *wh* islands:

(3) a ?Which problem do you wonder [how [PRO to solve t t]]
    b *How do you wonder [which problem [PRO to solve t t]]

• Obenauer's (1984) pseudo-opacity effects: In French a VP-initial adverbial QP selectively blocks extraction of certain VP-internal elements—for example, extraction of the direct object is possible, but extraction of the specifier of the direct object is not, as in (4).

(4) a   Combien de livres a-t-il beaucoup consultés t
        'How many of books did he a lot consult'
     b *Combien a-t-il beaucoup consulté [t de livres]
        'How many did he a lot consult of books'

• Ross's (1983) inner islands: Adverbial elements cannot be
extracted from the scope of negative operators, as (5) shows.

(5) a   Bill is here, which they (don't) know t
     b Bill is here, as they (*don't) know t

The striking similarity among these three cases is that the class of
possible extractions is, by and large, defined in the same way: an
argument can be extracted, an adjunct cannot. A unified account seems
to be in order. As a first approximation we could reason in the following way: Certain operators create a selective opaque domain for
adjunct variables; i.e., in the context of (6) adjunct variables cannot
be free in the domain of the operator.

(6) . . . [OP . . . _____ . . .] . . .

Of course, the empirical effects of this opacity principle would overlap
to a significant extent with the effects of the ECP, thus suggesting a
unification. But standard assumptions on the ECP module, and rigid
minimality in particular, do not seem to allow the ECP to subsume
our descriptive scope constraint: why should an intervening VP initial
operator or negation block the required government relation in (4b)
and (5b)?

The basic goal of this chapter is to show that a unified treatment of
(3)–(5) is made possible by a symmetric theory of government and
minimality. We will also discuss cases in which relativized minimality
is less restrictive than standard minimality. In some such cases, the
reduced restrictiveness will turn out to yield desired empirical consequences (see the end of subsection 1.3.1). In chapter 2 we will go back
to other, more problematic cases involving Comp-trace effects.

1.2 Wh Islands

Huang (1982) noticed that extraction of an adjunct from a *wh* island
gives a notably worse result than extraction of a complement, and
made the influential proposal of assimilating this asymmetry to familiar
subject-object asymmetries under the ECP. Consider the following
paradigm:

(7) a ??Which problem do you wonder how John could solve t t
    b *Which student do you wonder how t could solve the
       problem t
    c *How do you wonder which problem John could solve t t
(8) a Which problem do you think [t [John could solve t]]
    b Which student do you think [t [t could solve this problem]]
    c How do you think [t [John could solve this problem t]]

How can one express the fact that subjects and adjuncts pattern alike, and differently from complements, in this respect? The classical formulation of the ECP (Chomsky 1981) does not seem to draw the right distinction here:

(9) **ECP I:** A nonpronominal empty category must be
    (i) lexically governed, or
    (ii) antecedent-governed.

Manner adverbials are base-generated VP-internally, as is shown by the fact that they may be carried along under VP preposing (see Roberts 1988a):

(10) . . . and speak in this way he did

Therefore, they are lexically governed by V. Still, they appear to require antecedent government if (7c) is to be ruled out by the ECP. The same argument-adjunct asymmetry is found even with manner adverbials which are obligatorily selected by certain verbs:

(11) a ??With whom do you wonder [how [PRO to behave t t]]
     b *How do you wonder [with whom [PRO to behave t t]]

There can be little doubt, in this case, that the adjunct (or its trace) is lexically governed by the verb that selects it. If (9) is correct, why should antecedent government be required? The classical formulation of the ECP is insufficient here.

Stowell's (1981) proposal that the first clause of the ECP should refer to Theta government (government by a Theta assigner) appears more promising:

(12) **ECP II:** A nonpronominal empty category must be
    (i) Theta-governed, or
    (ii) antecedent-governed.

In (7a) the object trace is governed by the verb that assigns a Theta role to it; hence, it is Theta-governed, the ECP is fulfilled, and the weak deviance of the structure is solely determined by a Subjacency violation. In (7b) the subject trace is neither antecedent-governed nor Theta-governed (the verb does not govern the subject); hence, the structure is ruled out by the ECP. Huang's influential insight was that (7c) should be ruled out on a par with (7b) by the ECP. In fact, the adjunct trace is not Theta-marked; hence, the first clause of the ECP cannot be fulfilled, nor is it antecedent-governed in this structure; thus the ECP, as formulated in (12), is violated. On the contrary, examples (8b) and (8c) are well formed because the trace in the specifier of Comp antecedent governs the initial trace, and the second clause of the ECP is satisfied. (11b) can be excluded on a par with (7c) if we make the assumption that lexical selection of an adverbial does not involve Theta marking of the appropriate kind, which is restricted to referential expressions.[2]

Of course, in order to achieve this result, our theory of government must state that the *wh* phrase in the main Spec of Comp in (7b), (7c), and (11b) is too far away to directly antecedent-govern a trace in the lower clause, whereas the trace in the embedded COMP in (8b) and (8c) is close enough to do so. Keeping the discussion at an informal level for the moment, we can now see how Relativized Minimality gives us the desired result. Consider the informal characterization given in the introduction. In (7b) and (7c) a potential antecedent governor for the subject or adjunct trace is the operator in the lower Spec of Comp. This element is not an actual antecedent governor (in fact it is not an actual antecedent, there being no coindexation), but its presence suffices to block government from the actual antecedent: given Relativized Minimality, antecedent government cannot take place inside the domain of a potential antecedent governor. Since in (7b) and (7c) the relevant trace is not Theta-governed either, the ECP is violated. In (8b) and (8c), on the other hand, the non-Theta-governed trace is antecedent-governed by the trace in the embedded Spec of Comp; hence, the ECP is satisfied. In general, the combined effect of the ECP and Relativized Minimality on traces that are not Theta-governed is that the closest potential antecedent governor must be the *actual* antecedent governor; otherwise the ECP will be violated.

Concerning the well-formedness of (8c), one should raise the question why the subject (or the object) does not count as a potential antecedent governor for the adjunct trace: if it did, it would induce a minimality effect and hence an ECP violation. Clearly, what is needed is a selective definition of the notion "potential antecedent governor" such that an operator in the specifier of Comp counts as a potential antecedent governor for a *wh* trace but other clause-internal c-commanding positions do not count. And, of course, we need precise definitions of all the principles and notions involved.

1.3   Relativized Minimality

First of all, we must define the two types of government which the system uses:

(13) **Head Government**: X head-governs Y iff
    (i) X ∈ {A, N, P, V, Agr, T}
    (ii) X m-commands Y
    (iii) no barrier intervenes
    (iv) Relativized Minimality is respected.

(14) **Antecedent Government**: X antecedent-governs Y iff
    (i) X and Y are coindexed
    (ii) X c-commands Y
    (iii) no barrier intervenes
    (iv) Relativized Minimality is respected.

The two definitions are fully parallel. They differ in the characterization of the classes of governors: head governors are the lexical heads and some functional heads, at least those containing the agreement and tense specification (we will assume here that Agr and T can head independent projections and can also be associated as features with other heads); antecedent governors are coindexed categories. Both definitions involve a command requirement, to exclude upward government.[3] Both definitions include some notion of barrier, in the sense of Chomsky 1986b. Clearly, there is some tension between the Relativized Minimality idea and the notion of barrier, in that the former directly subsumes some of the cases dealt with by the latter in Chomsky's system. We will not fully explore the consequences of this tension here; in particular, we will not try to assess its implications for the important project of unifying in part the theories of government and bounding, and we will limit the comparison with Chomsky's (1986b) system to the domain of the theory of government. For our current purposes it will be sufficient to assume that XP's which are not directly selected by [+V] elements are inviolable barriers for government (see note 6), and we will not address the question of how subjacency barriers are to be characterized.

We then define Relativized Minimality through the variable notion "α-government," ranging over head government and antecedent government, as in (15).

(15) **Relativized Minimality**: X α-governs Y only if there is no Z such that
   (i) Z is a typical potential α-governor for Y,
   (ii) Z c-commands Y and does not c-command X.

The second clause of the principle simply defines "intervention" in hierarchical terms, rather than in linear terms as in our initial intuitive characterization.[4] As for the first clause of (15), we now have to define the notion "typical potential α-governor." The intuitive idea is that a typical potential α-governor for an element Y is a base-generated position that could bear the relevant kind of government relation to Y. For the moment I will leave this notion at an intuitive level, and will simply list the different subcases. A formal unification is offered in the second appendix of this chapter. As for the head government subcase, things are quite straightforward:

(16) Z is a typical potential head governor for Y = Z is a head m-commanding Y.

As for antecedent government, we assume, with Chomsky (1986b, p. 17) that this notion is a property of chains; it is then natural to distinguish three subcases, depending on whether Y is a trace in an A-chain (NP movement), in an A'-chain (*wh* movement), or in an X^0-chain (head movement):

(17) a Z is a typical potential antecedent governor for Y, Y in an A-chain = Z is an A specifier c-commanding Y.
   b Z is a typical potential antecedent governor for Y, Y in an A'-chain = Z is an A' specifier c-commanding Y.
   c Z is a typical potential antecedent governor for Y, Y in an X^0-chain = Z is a head c-commanding Y.

That is to say, minimality effects are exclusively triggered by potential governors of the different kinds filling base-generated positions: heads for head government and (respectively) A specifiers, A' specifiers, and heads for antecedent government in A, A', and X^0 chains. One will notice here a certain similarity with the Theory of Binding, in particular with the Generalized Binding approach (Aoun 1985, 1986). The classical insight behind the Specified Subject Condition and many more recent formulations of the Theory of Binding is that subjects (A specifiers) have a critical role in determining opaque domains for A anaphora: an anaphor must be bound in the domain of the closest A specifier, and not necessarily in the domain of the closest potential A antecedent; an A specifier seems to be the typical antecedent for an anaphor (the only possible antecedent in some languages), and as such it determines an opaque domain. Relativized Minimality, in a sense, generalizes this idea to government relations: typical potential governors of different kinds create impermeable domains for government. A close conceptual analogy also exists with Burzio's (1989) approach to cross-linguistic variation with respect to the Theory of Binding. According to Burzio, the class of elements which block binding relations and the class of possible antecedents are equivalent and are structured along an identical hierarchy of strength (a stronger potential antecedent is a stronger block, and so on). The analogies with the theory of binding look more than superficial, and suggest the possibility of a partial unification of government and binding along these lines, an important issue that I will not address here. See chapter 6 of Kayne 1984 for relevant discussion. The second appendix of this chapter capitalizes on the analogies between government and binding to attempt a formal unification of (16) and (17).

The next four subsections will show how the system works for antecedent government in A'-chains, A-chains, and X^0-chains, and for head government.

1.3.1 A'-Chains

Let us now go back to structures like the following:

(18) *How do you wonder [which problem [PRO to solve t t']]

Here the A' specifier *which problem* intervenes between *how* and its trace t', an A'-chain. Hence, by Relativized Minimality, t' is not antecedent-governed; it is not Theta-governed either, and therefore the structure is ruled out by the ECP. Notice that the same result holds if movement of *how* can proceed through VP adjunction, as in the system of Chomsky 1986b, and even if adjunction to IP is allowed as an intermediate step for *wh* movement. The relevant representation would be (19).

(19) How do you [t' [wonder [which problem [t" [PRO to [t'''
      [solve t t'''']]]]]]]

Here t is Theta-governed, and t'''', t''', and t' are antecedent-governed, but t" is not: t' is too far away because a potential A' governor, the *wh* operator in the spec of the embedded C, intervenes. In general, extraction of an adjunct from a *wh* island always gives rise to an ECP violation under Relativized Minimality: no matter how many intermediate traces there are, and where they are, an adjunct chain will include a link (which is (t',t'') in (19)) crossing the A' specifier of the embedded C, hence violating the ECP. So, for this class of cases, the stipulation that IP is not a possible adjunction site for *wh* movement (see Chomsky 1986b) can be dispensed with. (See Frampton 1989 for an elegant alternative approach, closer to Chomsky's original system, that also avoids this stipulation.)

Now consider (20).

(20) How do you think [t' that [Bill solved it t'']]

Here three heads (V, I, and C) and one A specifier (the subject) intervene between t' and t'' and between *how* and t''. Nevertheless, they do not interfere with antecedent government, as we now expect. Here Relativized Minimality is clearly superior to Rigid Minimality, which, unless special provisos are added, predicts that the relevant antecedent-government relations should be blocked by the intervening heads.

In the system of Chomsky 1986b the intervention of V^0 is nullified by the option of not projecting the V' level, which is crucial for minimality to apply in that system (see note 1). The intervention of I^0 is nullified by the assumption that the I system is intrinsically defective with respect to the theory of government in that its projections never count as inherent or minimality barriers. The intervention of C^0 realized as *that* is made irrelevant by the option of deleting *that* in the syntax of LF (and checking antecedent government for adjuncts at LF), along the lines of Lasnik and Saito's (1984) proposal. As for the intervention of a C^0 realized as an inflected auxiliary, the problem is not directly addressed in Chomsky 1986b; one could explore the possibility that this particular instance of I-to-C movement is a PF phenomenon, and as such does not interfere with the ECP (but see below for arguments against this view). Each of these problems, considered individually, looks solvable, and the proposed solutions may very well be tenable and plausible. Still, if we consider these cases jointly, the important question arises of why four independent factors should conspire to give the result that an intervening head never blocks antecedent government in the adjunct system.[5]

It appears reasonable to look at things from a different perspective: there is no conspiracy, it simply is the case that, in general, different kinds of government do not interfere with one another. This is the guiding intuition of the current approach. In (20) the relevant relation involves an A'-chain; hence, under relativized minimality, the intervening heads and A specifiers do not have any blocking power. The same is true of the antecedent-government relation between *how* and t'. In general, intervening heads and A specifiers never interfere with antecedent government in A'-chains.[6]

1.3.2 A-Chains

The fundamental case to consider under this rubric is the impossibility of SuperRaising:

(21) *John seems that it is likely [t to win]

Here the trace should be antecedent-governed, but it is not under Relativized Minimality: the intervening A specifier *it* blocks the government relation between *John* and its trace, and hence the structure violates the ECP. In this system we do not expect intervening heads to ever interfere with antecedent government in A-chains; in fact, an intervening V^0 and I^0 do not:

(22) John does not seem [t to be here]

Here again Rigid Minimality is forced to resort to special provisos, unnecessary under the current approach.[7] We also do not expect intervening A' specifiers to interfere. This is correct if the negation in (22) occupies an A' spec position, as will be argued below. The same conclusion holds for (23), given the evidence (to be provided below) that *beaucoup* occupies an A' specifier position.

(23) Ce livre a été beaucoup consulté t
     'This book was a lot consulted'

Strictly speaking, under the formulation (12) of the ECP the well-formedness of (23) does not establish the point that antecedent government holds in that structure: the passive trace is Theta-governed by the verb, and this suffices under formulation (12). But it will be shown in chapter 3, following Chomsky's (1986b) discussion, that antecedent government must hold in passive structures (see sections 3.4 and 3.6 in particular).

1.3.3 X^0-Chains

Here the descriptive generalization to be captured is the Head Movement Constraint, the fact that a moved head cannot skip an intervening head between its base position and its landing site (Travis 1984; Chomsky 1986b; Baker 1988); movement to C^0 can give (24b) but not (24c) from a basic structure like (24a).

(24) a   They could have left
     b   Could they t have left?
     c   *Have they could t left?

The moved X^0 antecedent-governs its trace in (24b), but not in (24c) because of the intervening I^0 in the latter case. The subject, an A specifier, does not interfere here, nor does the A' specifier *beaucoup* in the case of V-to-I movement in French illustrated by (25b).

(25) a   Jean a [beaucoup dormi]
       'Jean has a lot slept'
     b   Jean dort [beaucoup t]
       'Jean sleeps a lot'

In this case Relativized Minimality and Rigid Minimality give the same result.

1.3.4 Head Government

Minimality effects of head government can be illustrated through Case Theory. The most significant case is the fact that Exceptional Case Marking cannot take place across a CP level, and PRO is allowed to occur:

(26) a   *John tried [C^0 [Bill to win]]
     b   *John wonders [how C^0 [Bill to win]]

Whenever a CP is present, a C^0 (overt or null) must be present. It intervenes between the external governor–Case assigner and the lower subject in (26); hence, it blocks government and Case assignment. Here the tension between an approach to locality via barriers and one via minimality (rigid or relativized) becomes apparent. We have obtained the effect that government of a subject is always blocked across a CP, but this does not require treating CP as a barrier in these cases (inherently or through inheritance, as in Chomsky 1986b): the intervening C^0 suffices to determine the effect through minimality.[8]

1.4 Pseudo-Opacity

This section is based largely on important work by Hans Obenauer on various *wh* constructions in French (see, in particular, Obenauer 1976, 1984). The first relevant property of French is that the *wh* quantifier *combien* (how much/many), when used as an NP specifier, can pied-pipe the NP or be extracted from it:

(27) a [Combien de livres] a-t-il consultés t
         'How many of books did he consult'
      b Combien a-t-il consulté [t de livres]
         'How many did he consult of books'

This construction raises immediate questions about the nature of the Left Branch Constraint and its apparent violability. Here we will simply acknowledge the existence of such violations.[9]

The second relevant property of French is that it allows adverbial QP's to occur in VP-initial position:

(28) Il a beaucoup consulté ces livres
      'He has a lot/many times consulted these books'

This position can apparently be used as a landing site for movement of a QP specifier of the object NP:

(29) a Il a consulté [beaucoup de livres]
         'He has consulted many of books'
      b Il a beaucoup consulté [t de livres]
         'He has many consulted of books'

It is not really crucial for us to determine whether (29b) is derived through actual movement from a representation like (29a).[10]

These two properties are related in an interesting way, Obenauer points out. If the VP-initial position is filled by an adverbial quantifier, then *wh* extraction of the specifier of the object gives rise to a deviant structure whereas extraction of the whole object is acceptable. Consider the examples in (30).

(30) a Combien de livres a-t-il beaucoup consultés t
         'How many books did he a lot consult'
      b *Combien a-t-il beaucoup consulté [t de livres]
         'How many did he a lot consult of books'

In order to exclude structures of this type, Obenauer introduces a principle requiring that empty categories be bound by the closest potential binder available. This is, of course, very close to the idea of relativized minimality, which has the property of reducing the local binding effect to the ECP. Why should such facts as (30) be reduced to the ECP? There is a double similarity between Obenauer's pseudo-opacity and Huang's *wh* islands which strongly supports the idea of a unified account. First of all, extraction of (NP specifier) *combien* from a *wh* island gives rise to a strong violation, comparable to adjunct extraction and much worse than extraction of the whole direct object:

(31) a ?Combien de problèmes sais-tu [comment[PRO résoudre t t]]
     'How many of problems do you know how to solve'
   b *Combien sais-tu [comment[PRO résoudre [t de problèmes] t]]
     'How many do you know how to solve of problems'

Second, a VP-initial adverbial QP blocks not only extraction of the specifier of the direct object but also extraction of ordinary VP adjuncts:

(32) a Comment a-t-il résolu [beaucoup de problèmes] t
     'How did he solve many of problems'
   b *Comment a-t-il beaucoup résolu [t de problèmes] t
     'How has he many solved of problems'

These cases appear, in fact, to have the same status as Obenauer's examples.

How can this parallelism be represented by the theory? Notice, first of all, that the adjunct status of an NP specifier follows immediately from the definition of the ECP in (12). Consider (31). In (31a), a direct object is extracted; hence, the trace is Theta-governed by the verb and the ECP is fulfilled. The slightly degraded status of the sentence is presumably to be attributed to bounding theory, or to whatever property makes interrogative extraction out of an indirect question awkward in many languages. In (31b), the specifier obviously is not Theta-marked; hence, it is not Theta-governed. The only possibility for a specifier trace to satisfy the ECP is for it to be antecedent-governed, but this option is excluded in (31b) by Relativized Minimality; hence, the structure is ruled out by the ECP, as desired.

Consider now (30b) and (32b). Given minimal X'-theoretic assumptions, the VP-initial QP is the A' specifier of the VP.[11] In parallel with the other major case of an A' specifier, the specifier of C, this position is a possible scope position for quantifiers of a designated kind (*wh* operators for the Spec of C, adverbial quantifiers for the Spec of V), and is apparently available as a landing site for A' movement (or A' construal—see note 10). Then, a VP-initial QP meets our definition of potential antecedent governor in A'-chains for relativized minimality. In (30b) and (32b), the fact that the traces of *combien* and *comment* cannot be A'-governed by their actual antecedents is due to relativized minimality. They are not Theta-governed either; hence, the ECP is violated. In (30a), the object trace is Theta-governed by the verb, and the structure is well formed. We thus have the desired unified account of the two empirical domains under the ECP.[12]

Example (32b) should be contrasted with (33), which is acceptable.

(33) Pourquoi a-t-il beaucoup résolu de problèmes?
    'Why has he many solved of problems?'

At first sight, this asymmetry between *comment* and *pourquoi* with respect to pseudo-opacity is surprising, as both elements are strongly nonextractable from *wh* islands. A closer look at the level of attachment immediately clarifies things. (33) is acceptable because *pourquoi* differs from *comment* in that it is not a VP adverbial, and hence it is not extracted from the domain of *beaucoup* (perhaps it is not extracted at all—see section 2.4.), and no ECP violation arises.

Obenauer (1984, p. 173) points out an additional surprising asymmetry: if *de livres* is pronominalized by *en* and moved to the inflected verb in (30b), the structure appears to improve (even though it remains deviant for many speakers). Consider (34).

(34) Combien en a-t-il beaucoup consultés?
    'How many of-them-has he a lot consulted?'

Why should cliticization of *en* improve things? The behavior of past-participle agreement suggests that (34) and (30b) differ structurally in a significant way:

(35) a Combien a-t-il conduit de voitures?
      'How many did he drive of cars?'
   b Combient en a-t-il condui*tes*?
      'How many of-them-did he drive (+Agr)?

Agreement is possible in (35b) but not in (35a). We continue to follow Kayne's (1985) approach, according to which past-participle agreement is triggered when the direct object passes through an NP position higher than the past participle. This position cannot be the Spec of VP—already filled in (34)—so presumably it is the specifier of an object-agreement morpheme, or is adjoined to the projection of such a morpheme, essentially along the lines of Chomsky 1988. For concreteness we will call it the "Object-Agreement Position" (on which see also Belletti 1989). This analysis creates the option of a well-formed derivation for (34). Starting from a D-structure like (36a), the whole object NP first moves to the object-agreement position in (36b), thus bypassing the VP specifier; then, in (36c), the object-agreement position is vacated by clitic movement of *en* and *wh* movement of *combien*:

(36) a COMP Il a NP [beaucoup consulté [combien en]]

    b COMP Il a [combien en] [beaucoup consultés t]

    c Combien il en a [t′ t″] [beaucoup consultés t]

t, an argument trace, is Theta-governed and hence well formed, t′ is antecedent-governed by *combien*, and t″ is antecedent-governed by *en*. Thus, the Spec of VP does not intervene between *combien* and its trace, and the structure is well formed. This derivational option is not available for (30b), in which *combien* is directly extracted from the object position and hence cannot antecedent-govern its trace across the VP specifier.[13] Two differences between (35a) and (35b) with respect to pseudo-opacity and past-participle agreement can thus receive a uniform account.

1.5 Inner Islands

Ross (1983) noticed that negation interferes with extraction of adverbial elements but leaves unaffected the extractability of arguments. A striking minimal pair is the following (adapted from Ross 1983):

(37) a   Bill is here, which they (don't) know

    b *Bill is here, as they (*don't) know

wh movement of the adverbial element *as* is affected by the presence of negation, whereas movement of the argumental (proclausal) element *which* is not in the nearly synonymous sentence (37a).[14]

    Similar contrasts hold quite systematically (Travis 1984; Kayne 1986, note 17):

(38) a It is for this reason that I believe that John was fired

    b It is for this reason that I don't believe that John was fired

(38a) is ambiguous; the clefted adverbial can be construed with the main clause or with the embedded clause. (38b) is not ambiguous; the negation on the main verb blocks the lower construal (that is, the sentence cannot mean "this is the reason such that I don't believe that

John was fired for this reason," and can mean only "this is the reason which motivates my disbelief").

The same effect can be detected in simple clauses:

(39) a John was not fired for this reason
     b It is for this reason that John was not fired

In (39a) the adverbial PP can be interpreted inside or outside the scope of negation ("not for this reason John was fired" and "John was not fired, and this happened for this reason"). When the adverbial is clefted, only the external reading survives; that is, (39b) cannot mean "this is the reason that didn't motivate John's firing." As Ross points out for similar cases, the internal reading remains impossible if a context is set up which would make it pragmatically plausible (for example, if there were *a priori* three potential motivations, and I wanted to stress that one wasn't actually involved in John's firing, I could still not use (39b) to express this). This seems to be valid in general for the sentences discussed in this section.

The same effect is found, at a somewhat variable degree, with other types of adverbials—for instance, measure phrases. The examples in (40) are due to Bill Ladusaw.

(40) a How strongly do you believe that inflation will rebound
     b How strongly do you not believe that inflation will rebound

(40a) allows both main and embedded construal: the question can be about the strength of the belief or of inflation's rebound. (40b) is unambiguous and solely concerns the extent of the (dis)belief.

The argument-adjunct asymmetry is clearly illustrated by the following examples:

(41) a What do you believe he weighed (last week)
     b What do you not believe he weighed (last week)

(41a) allows both "Potatoes" and "200 pounds" as possible answers; (41b) seems to naturally allow only the first answer, in the appropriate context (that is, the direct object of agentive *weigh* can be extracted from the domain of negation, whereas the adverbial measure phrase selected by stative *weigh* cannot).

Now consider manner adverbials:

(42) a John didn't fix the car in this way
     b ?It is in this way that John didn't fix the car

(43) a It is in this way that I think that John fixed the car
     b *It is in this way that I don't think that John fixed the car

Manner adverbials, contrary to cause adverbials, do not naturally allow external scope. That is, the natural interpretation of (42a) has the adverbial in the scope of negation; the external reading is marginally possible only if the negated VP is somehow interpretable as referring to a purposeful achievement: John didn't fix the car, and he managed to do so in this way. (42b) is marginally acceptable only in this unnatural reading. (43a) is unambiguously interpreted with the manner adverbial construed with the embedded verb, and (43b) is excluded by the intervening negation, which blocks the only possible construal.

Thus, negation appears to create opacity effects on adjunct variables, a state of affairs which is obviously reminiscent of our previous discussion of *wh* islands and pseudo-opacity.

If negation qualifies as a typical potential A′ binder (an A′ specifier), the inner-island effect can be reduced to the ECP through relativized minimality: if a non-Theta-marked element is extracted from the domain of negation, it will be unable to antecedent-govern its trace because of relativized minimality, and an ECP violation will result. The A′ binding nature of negation is particularly visible in French, where negation patterns on a par with uncontroversial A′ binders such as *wh* elements and adverbial QP's in licensing a null NP specifier:

(44) a Combien a-t-il lu [*e* de livres]
     'How many did he read of books'
   b Il a beaucoup lu [*e* de livres]
     'He has many read of books'
   c Il n'a pas lu [*e* de livres]
     'He has not read of books'

The analysis of clausal *pas/not* as specifiers is made plausible by the fact that they can function as specifiers of other projections: QP's (*pas beaucoup, pas tout = not much, not all*) and AP's (*Je croyais Marie pas capable de faire cela = I considered Marie not capable of doing this*). Consider also the quasi-idiomatic French construction *Pour pas qu'il le fasse, . . .* (in order not that he do it), where *pas* appears as C specifier.

What projection could sentential negation be a specifier of? French clearly shows that *pas* is not a spec of VP; in fact, it can co-occur with a spec of VP, in a fixed order (*beaucoup pas* is ill formed):

(45) Jean n'a pas beaucoup mangé
      'Jean has not a lot eaten'

This seems to require the articulated structure of inflectional projections argued for by Pollock (1989, preliminary version dated 1986), according to which Agreement and Tense head distinct functional projections, AgrP and TP (see also Moro 1988). Following Belletti 1989b and Chomsky 1988, we will assume that AgrP is the highest inflectional projection; thus, *ne*, on a par with the other nonsubject clitics, is attached to Agr^0, and *pas* is the specifier of the lower inflectional head T^0:[15]

(46) [$_{AgrP}$ Jean n'a [$_{TP}$ pas [$_{VP}$ beaucoup mangé]]]

Under this analysis, inner-island effects immediately follow from the ECP under Relativized Minimality. Consider the following case in French, illustrating the effects directly in terms of the scope interaction of *pas* and *beaucoup*:

(47) a Il n'a [pas [résolu [beaucoup de problèmes]]]
         'He has not solved many of problems'
      b Il n'a [pas [beaucoup résolu [*e* de problèmes]]]
         'He has not many solved of problems'

Both sentences are well formed. (47a) shows a scope ambiguity: it can mean "many problems are such that he did not solve them," or "not many problems are such that he solved them." On the other hand, (47b) is unambiguous and allows only the second reading, with *beaucoup* receiving internal scope. In other words, (48a) is a possible LF representation, whereas (48b) is not (t is the trace of LF movement applying on (47a) and (47b)).

(48) a   [beaucoup de problèmes] il n'a [pas [résolu t]]
      b *beaucoup il n'a [pas [t résolu [*e* de problèmes]]]

This is another instance of inner-island effect induced by negation, applying on LF movement in this case. In (48a) the trace of the object is theta-governed by the verb, and the ECP is fulfilled. In (48b) the trace of *beaucoup* in the spec of VP is not theta-governed; it should be antecedent-governed, but it is not under relativized minimality, because of the intervening *pas*. (48b) is then ruled out by the ECP, and the only well-formed LF associated to (48b) is the one in which *beaucoup* is not extracted from the domain of *pas*. If sentential negation is analyzed as an A′ specifier, all the other cases of inner islands discussed so far follow straightforwardly in the same way. Not surprisingly, sentential negation also affects the syntactic extractability of *combien*, as pointed out by Moritz (1989):

(49) *Combien n'a-t-il pas conduit [t de voitures]
     'How many did he not drive of cars'

This case is the exact syntactic equivalent of the LF representation (48b). The proposed analysis covers both cases.

Inner-island effects are apparently not limited to sentential negation. Other negative or negative-like operators give rise to a similar pattern. Consider the following contrasts:

(50) a It is for this reason that everyone believes that Bill was fired
     b It is for this reason that no one believes that Bill was fired

(51) a It is by lethal injection that many people believe that John
        was executed
     b *It is by lethal injection that few people believe that John
        was executed

(52) a It is for this reason that John believes that Bill was fired
     b It is for this reason that only John believes that Bill was
        fired

Judgments vary in strength and across informants, but the general tendency seems to be that the lower construal is possible in examples (50a), (51a), and (52a) but is very awkward or impossible in examples (50b), (51b), and (52b). For example, (50a) is ambiguous, whereas (50b) can mean only "This is the reason which motivates the fact that no one believes that Bill was fired," and not "This is the reason such that no one believes that Bill was fired for this reason." (51a) can be interpreted with the clefted adverbial construed with the embedded verb; this interpretation—the only possible interpretation in such cases—is not available in (51b); hence, the structure is deviant (this example was pointed out by Bill Ladusaw). In (52b) the lower construal (possible in (52)a) is excluded, and the only possible interpretation is "This is the reason which motivates the fact that only John believes that Bill was fired."

It would then seem that inner-island effects are determined by "affective" operators, in Klima's (1964) sense—that is, operators licensing negative-polarity items (see Ladusaw 1981 and Barwise and Cooper 1981 for a semantic characterization of the class). Nonaffective operators, such as *every* and *many*, do not trigger the effect. A particularly clear minimal pair was suggested by M. Rochemont:

(53) a Few people did anything
     b *A few people did anything

(54) a Why do few people think that Bill was fired?
     b Why do a few people think that Bill was fired?

(53) shows that *few* is an affective operator whereas *a few* is not. In fact, the long-distance construal of *why* appears to be possible across the latter but not across the former in (54).

A possible interpretation of this apparent generalization is suggested by the fact that only affective operators trigger subject-aux inversion (Liberman 1974):

(55) With no job / few jobs would Bill be happy

(56) *With some job / a few jobs would Bill be happy

Under current assumptions, Subject-Aux Inversion is amenable to I^0-to-C^0 movement, a particular case of head-to-head movement. It then appears to be the case that, in English, affective operators and only affective operators can move to the spec of C in the syntax. We will make the conjecture that this is the syntactic reflex of a more general LF property: the canonical scope position for affective operators is an A' specifier position (of Comp, and possibly of other categories as well). This is obviously the case for an important subclass of affective operators, *wh* quantifiers, whose scope position is the Spec of Comp. For nonaffective operators, we keep the standard assumption that their canonical scope position is created through adjunction to IP (and possibly to other categories; see May 1985).

Let us now compare the LF representations of (50a) and (50b) in the lower construal under these assumptions:

(57) *It is for this reason [$_{CP}$ no one [$_{IP}$ t believes [that Bill was fired t]]]

(58) It is for this reason [$_{CP}$ [$_{IP}$ everyone [$_{IP}$ t believes] that Bill was fired t]]]

Taking literally our definition of "Typical Potential Antecedent Governor in A'-chains," we can account for the difference through relativized minimality and the ECP: in (57) *no one* is an A' specifier and hence a potential antecedent governor intervening between the adverbial PP and its trace (a trace of its A'-chain). Hence, the trace will not be antecedent-governed, and the ECP will be violated. In (58) on the other hand, *everyone* does not meet the definition of potential antecedent governor in A'-chains, in that it is not a specifier but an adjunct.

Hence, relativized minimality is not triggered, and the A'-chain of the clefted adverbial does not violate the ECP.[16]

Simple negative questions such as (59) raise the issue of the LF position of the negative quantifier:

(59) What did no one say ?

One possibility that comes to mind is that the Spec of C can be multiply filled at LF by the *wh* element and the negative quantifier. In fact, the idea that nodes can be multiply filled at LF is not implausible, as the uniqueness of fillers at S-structure may be regarded as a consequence of the obligatory linearization at PF, a process that does not affect LF representations: multiply filled nodes cannot be properly linearized. Among other things, this would immediately account for the otherwise mysterious asymmetry between S-structure and LF that many languages manifest in multiple questions: at most one *wh* element is moved to Comp at S-structure, while all the *wh* elements presumably are in Comp at LF:

(60) **S-s:** I wonder [what [you gave t to whom]]
     LF: I wonder [what   [you gave t t]]
                       to whom

Whatever its general plausibility, two considerations strongly suggest that the option of multiply filling Spec of C at LF does not provide the solution of the problem raised by (59). First of all, the LF representation assigned to (59) would be indistinguishable from a superiority violation (*What did who say*). Whatever principle rules out superiority violations of this kind (see note 15 to chapter 2) would presumably exclude such a representation as well. Second, there is an inner-island effect in this case too. Example (61) does not allow the internal construal (What is the reason such that no one came for this reason?).

(61) Why did no one come ?

Now, if *no one* was in the same position as *why* at LF, it would not intervene between the latter and its trace in the relevant sense, and the internal construal would not be blocked in the familiar manner.

A more plausible hypothesis to cover cases such as (59) and (61) appears to be that the spec of IP can optionally count as an A' specifier at LF. In cases such as (59) this option must be taken to properly assign scope to the affective operator, as the spec of C is not available. (Even if we allow nodes to be multiply filled at LF, the representation obtained by moving *no one* to spec of C^0 would be ruled out by the

principle excluding superiority violations.) Thus, *no one* does not have
to move, and it determines the inner-island effect from its S-structure
position.[17]

Appendix 1   Negation and V-to-I Movement

The above discussion presupposes an analysis of the negative marker
as an A' specifier on the appropriate level(s) of representation. This
assumption is in conflict with various recent proposals according to
which the negative marker heads an autonomous projection, NegP
(negative phrase). From the perspective of the approach introduced
here, this alternative appears problematic, at least for such elements
as English *not* and French *pas*. (As is mentioned in note 15, our
approach is compatible with the NegP idea if *pas*, *not* is analyzed as
the specifier, rather than the head, of the negative phrase.) We have
seen that an intervening negation of this kind blocks A'-chains involving adjuncts. Reciprocally, it does not block X^0-chains. This is shown
by the possibility of V-to-I movement in the following cases:

(62) a They should [not have left]
     b They have [not t left]

(63) a Pour ne [pas manger]
     b Ils ne mangent [pas t]

On *have/be* Raising see Emonds 1976 and Lasnik 1981; these works
follow lines originally proposed by Edward Klima. On the French
case, see Emonds 1978 and Pollock 1989. Similarly, the Continental
Scandinavian languages offer particularly clear cases of head-to-head
movement across a negative marker: the tensed verb follows the negative marker in embedded clauses, whereas it precedes the negative
marker in main clauses (see Holmberg and Platzack 1988 and references
quoted there). Consider the following Swedish examples:

(64) a Jan   köpte   inte boken
        'Jan bought not   books'
     b . . . om Jan inte köpte   boken
        '. . . if Jan not bought books'

As main-clause word order is determined by Verb Second, the now
familiar analysis of such alternations involves the assumption that
(64b) manifests the basic word order, whereas (64a) is a V-2 structure
with the tensed verb in C^0 and another constituent (the subject in this

case) in its Spec. Clearly, this particular instance of head-to-head movement can move the verb across a negation marker here. It thus appears to be quite generally true that an intervening negation blocks antecedent government in A' chains but not in X^0-chains. If negation was a head, we would expect the opposite pattern, which is not attested.

Looking more closely, we must acknowledge a residual blocking effect of negation on an apparent X^0 dependency: negation appears to block the association of the inflectional morpheme with a lexical verb in English, as (65) illustrates.

(65) a   John smokes
      b   *John smokes not
      c   *John not smokes
      d   John does not smoke

There seems to be a general consensus on the assumption that a lexical verb is not allowed to move to an inflectional head in modern English, whence the ill-formedness of (65b) (Emonds 1976; Pollock 1989; Chomsky 1988); the well-formedness of (65a) then involves affix-hopping (Chomsky 1957), lowering the content of Infl to V in the VP, and the sentence has the following S-structure (Chomsky 1988):

(66) John $[_{I^0}$ t$]$ $[_{VP}$ [smoke+s]]

The ill-formedness of (65c) then seems to suggest that an intervening negation blocks affix hopping, and makes it necessary to insert the dummy auxiliary *do* in Infl to ensure morphological well-formedness. We thus seem to reach a rather paradoxical conclusion: an intervening negation does not affect the regular V-to-I movement of (62)–(64), but it blocks I-to-V movement (affix hopping). Why should this be so? Different answers are suggested by the different possible approaches to a more fundamental question: Why is a downgrading application of head-to-head movement allowed in (66)? Chomsky (1988) proposes that an upgrading movement of the inflected verb in the syntax of LF rescues the structure. Consider the following adaptation of Chomsky's proposal (an analogous approach is independently proposed by M. R. Manzini in forthcoming work). We will assume that whatever constraint blocks V-to-I movement in the syntax, it is still operative at LF; hence, in (66) the inflected verb cannot cover the trace of Infl at LF. But the verb is now assigned the tense specification, a specification often regarded as operator-like. It is then natural to assume that the inflected verb can undergo operator movement, a familiar LF process, adjoining it to some I projection. The LF representation of (66) would then be (67).

(67) John $[_{V^0}$ [smoke]+[s]] $[_{I^0}$ t] $[_{VP}$ $[_{V^0}$ t]]

This is a well-formed representation, with both traces properly bound and governed by their antecedents. The inflection -*s* governs the Infl trace (assuming that the intervening V boundary does not block the required command relation; in fact, X^0 boundaries never do if the command relations are defined in terms of "projection," as in note 3; see also Baker's (1988) Government Transparency Corollary); moreover, the inflected verb and the verbal trace now form an A'-chain, created by operator movement; therefore, the intervening I^0 does not block the antecedent-government relation under Relativized Minimality.

An important consequence of this analysis is that it immediately explains why an intervening negation blocks structures like (65c): if syntactic lowering of Infl can be salvaged by LF operator movement of the tensed verb, we expect the corresponding A' dependency to be affected by an intervening negation, as A' dependencies generally are. Thus, in the LF representation (68) the verbal trace cannot be antecedent-governed by its A' antecedent, the inflected verb; therefore ECP is violated, and (65c) is correctly ruled out.[18, 19]

(68) John $[_{V^0}$ [smoke]+[s]] $[_{I^0}$ t] not $[_{VP}$ $[_{V^0}$ t]]

Appendix 2   Government Theory Compatibility

The system of definitions of section 1.3 specifies the different subcases of the crucial notion *typical potential α governor* and expresses the unitary nature of these cases only at an intuitive level. The purpose of this appendix is to present a slightly more refined system of definitions in which the four subcases are formally unified. I will draw on the conceptual and formal similarity between government and binding, and achieve the desired unification through an extension of Chomsky's (1986a) notion *Binding Theory compatibility* to Government Theory. Let us first rephrase the definitions of the different kinds of government by sharpening certain distinctions that were partly implicit in the initial characterizations. In particular, we will now assume that each definition must specify some *configurational conditions*, the tree geometry in which the relation can hold, some *substantive condition* that an element must satisfy to qualify as a governor, and some *locality con-*

ditions. Once this tripartite distinction is made, the definition of head-government takes the following shape:

(69) **Head Government**: X head governs Y iff
    (i) a. X is a head
       b. X m-commands Y
    (ii) X = {[$\pm$V $\pm$N], Agr, T}
    (iii) a. no barrier intervenes
        b. Relativized Minimality is respected

(i) and (iii) express the configurational and locality conditions, respectively; (ii) expresses the substantive condition: a head-governor must be endowed with some special property, lexical content or T or Agr.

As for antecedent government, I agree with Chomsky (1986b, p. 17) that this notion is a property of chains; thus, it is natural to assume that antecedent government splits into three subcases, depending on the kind of chain involved:

(70) **Antecedent Government**: X W-antecedent governs Y (W = {A, A', X^0}) iff
    (i) a. X is in a W-position
       b. X c-commands Y
    (ii) X and Y are coindexed
    (iii) a. no barrier intervenes
        b. Relativized Minimality is respected.

W is a variable ranging over A, A', and X^0 antecedent government, the three subcases corresponding to chains formed by NP movement, *wh* movement, and head movement. The substantive condition on antecedent government is that X and Y are coindexed categories (see (70ii); but see section 3.6 for a modification required by the theory of indices developed in chapter 3). The locality conditions (iii) are identical in (69) and (70), and can be factored out. The new definitions differ from (13) and (14) in that the distinction between purely configurational conditions and substantive conditions is clearly stated, and the three subcases of antecedent government are overtly expressed.

In approaching the definition of relativized minimality, we can now consider the variable notion α-*government* as ranging over the four cases expressed by (69) and (70), head government, and the three subcases of antecedent government (A-antecedent government, A'-antecedent government, and X^0-antecedent government). The intuitive idea is that a particular kind of government is blocked by the intervention of an element which typically has the potential for government of that kind. The four subcases of typical potential governor are repeated in (16) and (17) for ease of reference.

(16)   Z is a typical potential head governor for Y = Z is a head m-commanding Y

(17) a Z is a typical potential antecedent governor for Y, Y in an A-chain = Z is an A specifier c-commanding Y

   b Z is a typical potential antecedent governor for Y, Y in an A'-chain = Z is an A' specifier c-commanding Y

   c Z is a typical potential antecedent governor for Y, Y in an X^0-chain = Z is a head c-commanding Y.

The next step is to formally unify these cases. We can now take direct advantage of the close conceptual analogy with the theory of binding stressed in section 1.3. In Chomsky's (1986a) approach, the locality conditions on binding are determined in part by the virtual satisfiability of the Binding Principle: the Governing Category of an element is a domain virtually allowing an indexation *Binding Theory compatible*, i.e., a domain in which the configurational properties for Binding are satisfied, while the substantive property (actual indexation) need not be. We can think of the locality conditions on government in essentially the same way. We continue to assume that the theory of government consists of the four subcases defined by (69) and (70). We then say that an element Z is α-*Government Theory compatible* (α-GT compatible) with an element Y when the configurational conditions (i) for the appropriate subcase of government are met (categorial status and position of the governor, command), while the substantive condition (ii) on the nature of the governor need not be (actual coindexation for antecedent government, actual possession of the governing quality for head government). (It is immaterial for the present purposes whether the locality conditions enter into the definition of GT compatibility or not.) Thus, for instance, a head is head-GT compatible with an element it m-commands, whether or not it is endowed with actual governing force; an A-specifier is A-antecedent GT compatible with an element it c-commands, whether or not it is actually coindexed with this element; etc. It should now be clear that α-GT compatibility encompasses the different types of typical potential governors. We can then write the following principle.

(71) **Relativized Minimality**: X α-governs Y only if there is no Z such that

  (i) Z is a base-generated position

  (ii) Z is α-GT compatible with Y

  (iii) Z c-commands Y and does not c-command X.

Clause i is intended to limit the blocking effect to heads and specifiers, as adjoined positions do not seem to have this capacity (see section 1.5, in particular, for empirical evidence showing this point). Clause iii expresses the intervention in hierarchical terms, as before. Clause ii unifies the four cases of typical potential governors of (16) and (17) under the notion GT compatibility, obviously reminiscent of Chomsky's BT compatibility.

In conclusion: A significant parallelism is drawn between government and binding in that in both theories locality is (partially) defined by the occurrence of a structural configuration that fulfills the geometric conditions on the relevant relation, irrespective of whether or not this configuration also fulfills the substantive conditions (actual coindexation, etc.).

Chapter 2
A Conjunctive Formulation
of the ECP

2.1 Introduction

The bulk of this chapter is devoted to an analysis of *that*-trace effects. The existence of such effects raises an acute problem for the approach developed in the first chapter, which excludes in principle the possibility that an intervening C^0 may block an antecedent-government relation. We are then led to adopt a conjunctive formulation of the ECP such that a trace must simultaneously fulfill a head-government requirement and an identification requirement (which may be fulfilled via antecedent government). Section 2.2 shows how *that*-trace effects can be analyzed as violations of the head-government requirement. Section 2.3 is devoted to an extensive exploration of the consequences of the head-government requirement in different syntactic domains, and to the determination of the proper formal definition of the requirement. Section 2.4 illustrates how different types of adjunct traces can fulfill the two clauses of conjunctive ECP. Section 2.5 deals with the technique that many languages use to allow proper head government of subject traces in cases of permissible extraction. This technique is shown to be amenable to a well-defined formal operation: specifier-head agreement in the domain of Comp. Section 2.6 illustrates other devices offered by Universal Grammar to allow subject extraction, with particular reference to the technique available in Null Subject Languages. Section 2.7 deals with the apparent absence of *that*-trace effects in relative clauses, and introduces a principled approach to the various manifestations of the so-called Doubly Filled Comp Effect.

2.2 *That*-Trace Effects

The following contrast gives a standard illustration of the *that*-trace effect:

(1) a   Who do you think [t' that [Bill saw t]]
    b *Who do you think [t' that [t left]]

The subject-object asymmetry suggests that ECP is involved. But how is antecedent government to be blocked in (1b)? The standard analysis of COMP, involving only one position, provided an immediate answer: t' could not antecedent-govern t because the c-command requirement on government was not fulfilled:

(2)

$$
\begin{array}{c}
\text{S'} \\
\diagup \qquad \diagdown \\
\text{COMP} \qquad \quad \text{S} \\
\diagup \ \diagdown \qquad \quad \diagup \\
\text{t'} \quad \text{that} \qquad \text{t}
\end{array}
$$

Under the more sophisticated analysis of the complementizer projection of Chomsky 1986b, things are less straightforward: t' is the specifier, *that* is the head of C, and hence the c-command relations are not affected:

(3)

$$
\begin{array}{c}
\qquad \text{CP} \\
\text{t'} \diagup \quad \diagdown \text{C'} \\
\qquad \text{C} \diagup \ \diagdown \\
\qquad | \qquad \text{IP} \\
\qquad \text{that} \quad \text{t}
\end{array}
$$

At first sight, rigid minimality appears to be more promising in this case: under rigid minimality the intervening head *that* could block antecedent government from t', whereas under relativized minimality this kind of interaction between different kinds of governors is unexpected. But the issue is more complex. First of all, the formulation of an empirically adequate version of rigid minimality raises technical problems: how come an overt complementizer blocks antecedent government whereas a null one does not? Consider (4).

(4) Who do you think [t' 0 [t left]]

The distinction is hard to make in a principled way (Chomsky 1986b, p. 47). A second problem is raised by the acceptability of sentences such as (5).

(5) How do you think [t' that [Bill solved the problem t]]

The fact that *that* does not determine an ECP violation on the adjunct trace and the fact that the subject-adjunct parallelism manifested in *wh* islands is broken here cast some *prima facie* doubts on the idea that an intervening overt complementizer can affect an antecedent-government relation. (See the discussion of this problem in chapter 1, and the references cited there.)

In recent years the possibility has often been explored that the usual disjunctive formulation of the ECP is to be replaced by a conjunctive formulation, according to which a nonpronominal empty category must simultaneously fulfill some requirement of both head government *and* antecedent government (Stowell 1981, 1985; Jaeggli 1982, 1985; Aoun, Hornstein, Lightfoot, and Weinberg 1987; Contrerars 1986; Torrego 1985; Chomsky 1986b; Koopman and Sportiche 1986, 1988). If the ECP module is developed along these lines, the possibility arises that examples like (1) are ruled out by a violation of the head-government requirement rather than by one of antecedent government. The relativized-minimality approach naturally leads us to explore this possibility. I will, then, assume that a trace must always fulfill a requirement of the following kind:

(6) A nonpronominal empty category must be properly head-governed.

It is now necessary to make clear what "properly" means in this context, and, more specifically, what kind of property can be appealed to in order to exclude (1).

The first idea that comes to mind is to keep in the new formulation the traditional insight of disjunctive ECP, according to which the lexical/nonlexical distinction is relevant here: if "properly" is understood in (6) as meaning "lexically," then (1) will be excluded because its head governor, Inflection, is not lexical. This idea has been influential throughout the development of the ECP module, but a very simple consideration suggests that it may not capture the right generalization. A whole VP can be topicalized across an overt C (Chomsky 1986b, p. 20):

(7) I asked John to go home, and [go home] I think [t' that [he did t]]

As Chomsky (1986b) and Roberts (1988b) point out, the contrast between subject and VP extraction remains detectable also when extraction takes place from an indirect question:

(8) a   I wonder whether John won the race
    b   *John, I wonder whether t won the race
    c   ?. . . and win the race I wonder whether he did t

In short, I can license t', but not t, in the following configuration:

(9)

Obviously, the lexical/nonlexical distinction is unable to capture this state of affairs. Others formal distinctions are immediately suggested by (9); see also Lobeck 1986 and Zagona 1988.

The intuition to be developed is that a complement is governed in a stronger way than a specifier, and that the head-government requirement on traces refers to such a stronger notion of government. Notice that in (9) the respective positions of t and t' differ both linearly and hierarchically with respect to I. There are then two major ways to phrase the relevant condition. The linear asymmetry recalls Kayne's (1984) notion of canonical government: I governs its complement, the VP, in the canonical direction in English (from left to right), while it governs the subject in the noncanonical direction. One could then assume that in (6) "properly" means "canonically": a trace must be governed in the canonical direction that the language chooses.[1] This possibility, explored in Stowell 1985, was adopted in a previous version of the present chapter (see also Longobardi 1987). Alternatively, one could exploit the hierarchical asymmetry and claim that a trace must be head-governed "within the immediate projection of the head," as is the case for t' but not for t in (57); "properly governed" would then mean "governed by X^0 within X'."

The most straightforward empirical difference between the two views concerns the licensing of a trace in the specifier position in cases in which specifier and complement are on the same side or on opposite sides of the head:

(10) a   [Spec [Compl X^0]]
     b   [Spec [X^0 Compl]]

The hierarchical definition predicts no difference between the two cases; in neither (10a) nor (10b) can a trace in Spec be governed within the immediate projection of the head phrase-internally; therefore, the structure can survive only if an external proper head governor is available. The linear definition predicts a clear difference: in (10a) the spec is canonically governed by X^0; hence, a spec trace would always have its proper-government requirement satisfied phrase-internally, so it should survive independent of the existence of an external governor, and one would predict a much freer extractability of the Spec in (10a) than in (10b), all other things being equal. The hierarchical definition thus is more restrictive, in that it predicts more limited and more uniform possibilities of specifier extraction across languages. (Whether or not there are also cases in which the definition in terms of canonical government is more restrictive depends on the specific definition of canonical government; consider the variants mentioned in the preceding note.) In the following discussion we will adopt the definition in terms of "government within the immediate projection," whose restrictive predictions on specifier extraction appear to be empirically justified (see subsections 2.3.2 and 2.3.5), but we will keep the alternative definition in mind, and will underscore the empirical cases in which the two definitions diverge. See Saito 1984 for an argument supporting the view, close to the one adopted here, that the head-government component of the ECP requires strict c-command.

Let us now state the Empty Category Principle in a conjunctive form. To phrase the idea within a somewhat broader theoretical context, we may think of the theory of each type of null element as consisting of two components: a principle of formal licensing, which characterizes the formal environment in which the null element can be found, and a principle of identification (I follow here Jaeggli's (1982) terminology), which recovers some contentive property of the null element on the basis of its immediate structural environment (see Rizzi 1986 for a detailed discussion in the context of the theory of null pronominals).

As for the identification requirement, we will initially keep Stowell's (1981, 1985) assumption that it can be fulfilled by government from an actual antecedent or by government from a Theta-marking head. The latter case can perhaps be reduced to the former,[2] but in our formulation we will keep the two options distinct for clarity of presentation:

(11) **ECP III:** A nonpronominal empty category must be
    (i) properly head-governed (Formal Licensing)
    (ii) antecedent-governed or Theta-governed (Identification).

Let us see how the system works if we combine the conjunctive formulation of the ECP and Relativized Minimality. In (1b), t′ antecedent-governs t, but the latter does not meet the proper-head-government requirement, regardless of whether the linear or the hierarchical definition is chosen: I does not govern t canonically or under its immediate projection I', and *that* (a head inert for government; see the definitions of head government in section 1.3 and appendix 2) does not govern t at all. Hence, the structure is ruled out by conjunctive ECP. In (8b) the subject trace is not properly head-governed; moreover, it is neither theta-governed nor antecedent-governed, and hence both clauses of the ECP are violated.

In (7) the VP trace is antecedent-governed by t' in Spec of C, and properly head-governed by I. In (8c) the VP trace is properly head-governed by Infl, but it is not antecedent-governed, owing to the intervention of the lower Spec of Comp; as the structure clearly does not instantiate an ECP violation comparable to adjunct extraction in the same context, we must tentatively conclude, with Chomsky (1986b), that I theta-governs the VP (but see note 17 of chapter 3). Both clauses of the ECP are thus fulfilled via government from I. Finally, in (5) the adjunct trace is antecedent-governed by the trace in the Spec of C and properly head-governed by V (or by T^0; see below). Hence, in the case of adjunct extraction the two clauses of the ECP are fulfilled separately, and the lack of *that*-trace effects is readily explained. (See Lasnik and Saito 1984 for a different approach to this problem.) All the cases of object extraction can be analyzed as in the preceding section. The verb now fulfills both requirements on the object trace (it properly head-governs and Theta-governs the position); therefore, object extraction never gives rise to an ECP violation.

A problem is raised by the fact that VP topicalization appears to be (marginally) possible also from untensed clauses:

(12) . . . and [fix the car], he tried [PRO to t]

If the infinitival inflection is inert for government, as is shown by the fact that PRO is allowed in its specifier, how can it properly head-govern the VP trace? A simple solution is offered by the current assumptions on the nature of infinitival projections (see chapter 1). If we assume, with Pollock (1989), that agreement and tense head independent functional projections, and if we admit, with Belletti (1988) and Chomsky (1988), that the Agr projection contains the T projection, we end up with the following clausal structure:

(13)

Agr is a governor only if it has features, i.e., in tensed clauses (and even in that case its governing capacities are restricted to the element(s) it agrees with (see below)). T^0, we may assume, is always a governor, as the sentence always has some tense specification (Motapanyane 1988). The apparent paradox raised by infinitival structures like (12) is then resolved: the specifier of Agr is ungoverned, as both its potential head governors, Agr^0 and C^0, are inert for government in infinitives; the VP is governed by T^0, and hence VP topicalization is allowed.[3]

We still have to deal with the acceptability of (4). Before turning to that, it is worthwhile to explore other consequences of the conjunctive formulation of the ECP.

2.3   Consequences of the Proper-Head-Government Requirement

2.3.1   Constraints on Heavy NP Shift
Postal (1974) pointed out that subjects cannot undergo Heavy NP Shift in English:

(14) a *[t are intelligent] all the students who can solve this problem
     b I would like to introduce t to Mary all the students who can
        solve this problem

The subject-object asymmetry strongly suggests that the ECP is involved, but the standard disjunctive formulation of this principle does not capture the contrast: the shifted NP should be able to antecedent-govern its trace. On the other hand, the system we have introduced makes the necessary distinction. (14)a is excluded by the ECP because the head-government requirement is not met: the highest inflectional head does not properly govern the subject trace (whether the linear or the hierarchical definition is chosen), and C (if it is there) does not govern it at all. The fact that the antecedent-government requirement is met does not suffice to rule in the representation.[4]

Conjunctive ECP predicts that if an independent proper governor is provided, heavy NP shift should successfully apply to a subject. The case is provided by Exceptional Case Marking environments:

(15) I believe [t to be intelligent] all the students who can solve this problem

Here the head-government requirement is fulfilled by *believe*, and the antecedent-government requirement is fulfilled by the shifted NP.

Kayne (1984, chapter 2) points out that Acc-ing structures do not allow Heavy NP Shift of the subject:

(16)   *I'd prefer [t studying linguistics] all the students who can solve this problem

In fact, there is evidence suggesting that in this construction the subject is governed internally by the gerundival inflection, and not by the main verb (Kayne 1984; Reuland 1983); for instance, the subject can receive accusative case in environments in which no external assigner is available:

(17) [Him studying linguistics] would be a waste of time

(17) is then excluded because the subject trace is not properly head-governed by its inflection.[5]

2.3.2   Extraction of Measure Phrase from AP

In English a measure phrase modifying an AP cannot be extracted, and pied-piping of the whole AP is the only option; in Italian both extraction and pied-piping are possible, the latter option being stylistically marked (as is often the case when extraction is possible) and restricted to special contexts such as that of (19b).

(18) a *How is he [t tall]
     b [How tall] is he t
(19) a Quanto è alto?
        'How is (he) tall?'
     b Sapevo che era alto, ma non immaginavo quanto alto potesse essere
        'I knew he was tall, but I didn't imagine how tall he could be'

(18a) can be excluded by the proper-head-government requirement of the ECP, along the following lines: the adjective governs its QP specifier, but not within its immediate projection; as such, it cannot fulfill the proper-government requirement of the QP trace; moreover, it blocks government of the QP trace from the copula under Minimality.[6]

Why should (19a) contrast sharply with (18a)? An analysis is immediately suggested by the normal answers to questions of this kind in the two languages:

(20) a He is [[two meters] tall]
     b E' [alto [due metri]]
        '(He) is tall two meters'

The measure phrase can occur to the right of the adjective in Italian, as an adjunct to the AP, and extraction appears to be possible with the following representation:

(21) Quanto è [alto t]?

That the measure phrase is within the AP (or adjoined to it) is shown by the fact that it can be left dislocated with the AP, as in (22a): that the postadjectival position can be filled by a *wh* measure phrase is shown by echo questions like (22b).

(22) a Alto due metri, non lo è di certo!
        'Tall two meters, he is not for sure'
     b Hai detto che il film è lungo QUANTE ORE?!
        'You said that the movie is long how many hours?'

The contrast between (18) and (19) immediately follows from the definition of proper government as canonical government: in (19), but not in (18), the trace of the measure phrase is canonically governed by the adjective. The contrast also follows from the hierarchical definition: if the postadjectival measure phrase is adjoined to AP, then its trace can be properly governed by the higher T^0—an option that does not arise in English, as the measure phrase is restricted to occur as the AP specifier.

Comparative considerations are relevant here. The adjectival specifier cannot be extracted in German (and Dutch), even though it is on the same (pre-head) side of the adjective as the complements:

(23) a [Wie lang] ist es?
        'How long is it?'
     b *Wie ist es [t lang]?
        'How is it long?'

This is expected if proper government is defined in hierarchical terms, whereas the definition in terms of canonical government, all other things being equal, would predict German and Dutch to differ from

English in this respect. In general, the systematic resistance that some SOV languages show against specifier extraction of various phrasal categories seems to provide an indication in favor of the more restrictive hierarchical definition of proper head government.

2.3.3 An Asymmetry between the Two Clauses of the ECP

The French clitic *en* can pronominalize an adnominal complement of the direct object, and it can also pronominalize the N' constituent of the direct object when the NP has an indefinite specifier:

(24) a On a publié [la première partie de ce livre]
        'They published the first part of this book'
     b On a publié [trois livres]
        'They published three books'

(25) a On en a publié [la première partie t]
        'They of-it published the first part'
     b On en a publié [trois t]
        'They of-them published three'

Both kinds of extraction are impossible from deep subjects:

(26) a *[La première partie t] en montre que. . .
        'The first part of-it-shows that. . . '
     b *[Trois t] en montrent que. . .
        'Three of-them-show that. . . '

This is expected; the downgrading extraction is excluded, as the trace of *en* is not c-commanded by its antecedent. Ruwet (1972, chapter 3) noticed that the two kinds of extraction behave differently in a restricted number of environments, in which the adnominal complement is extractable from a subject ("*en* avant") but the N' is not. Couquaux (1979) and Pollock (1986) observed that this asymmetry typically arises with derived subjects:

(27) a [La première partie t] en a été publiée t en 1985
        'The first part of-it-has been published in 1985'
     b *[Trois t] en ont été publiés t en 1985
        'Three of-them-have been published in 1985'

The asymmetry between (26a) and (27a) is plausibly to be attributed to reconstruction: the proper binding relation between *en* and its trace can be restored under reconstruction in the latter, but not in the former. Why is (27b) ill formed? Pollock (1986) proposes a binding-theoretic approach: If in general an NP and its subconstituent N' are coindexed, then the subject and *en* are coindexed in (27b); the pronominal *en* is therefore incorrectly bound in its Governing Category, and (27b) is ruled out by Binding Principle B; in (27a) the adnominal complement is referentially distinct from the subject, and hence no violation is determined. This ingenious approach conflicts with the natural assumption that the binding principles concern genuine referential dependencies and therefore apply only chain externally; it is also fundamentally incompatible with the restrictive use of referential indices introduced in the next chapter. An alternative is now offered by the conjunctive ECP: in (27a) the trace of *en* is properly head-governed by the noun; in (27b) it is not properly head-governed, and hence the structure is ruled out by the ECP module. (On the limited capacity of nouns with respect to proper head government, see appendix 2 of chapter 3 and the references cited there.) In (25) no asymmetry arises, because the N' trace within the direct object in (25b) can be head-governed by the verb. (The accessibility of heads to external governors, stipulated in Belletti and Rizzi 1981, now follows directly from the minimality principle, as is easy to verify.)

This analysis implies that the head-government requirement differs from the binding (and antecedent-government) requirement of a trace in that it cannot be satisfied under reconstruction; otherwise the head-government requirement could be satisfied by the verb on the "reconstructed" structure corresponding to (27b). The same conclusion is supported by the observation (Rizzi 1982b) that, in languages with fairly free cleft formation (e.g., Italian), control complements can be clefted but raising complements cannot:

(28) a E' [PRO lavorare di più] che Gianni vuole t
        'It is to work more that Gianni wants'
     b *E' [t lavorare di più] che Gianni sembra t'
        'It is to work more than Gianni seems'

It is natural to assume that (28b) is deviant because the subject trace is not properly head-governed, which implies that the required configuration cannot be restored by reconstruction.[7]

The same conclusion is also supported by a well-known asymmetry between raising and control complements in some Germanic languages, which closely mirrors (28). Although control complements can be found in both preverbal (VP internal) and extraposed position in German and Dutch, Raising complements can be found only in preverbal position (Koster 1984, 1987; Hoekstra 1984; Giusti 1988; the following German examples are from Giusti 1988):

(29) a   . . . weil Johann [PRO ein guter Kerl zu sein] versucht
         '. . . because Johann a good guy to be tries'
     b   . . . weil Johann t versucht [PRO ein guter Kerl zu sein]
         '. . . because Johann tries a good guy to be'
(30) a   . . . weil Johann [t ein guter Kerl zu sein] scheint
         '. . . because Johann a good guy to be seems'
     b *. . . weil Johann t' scheint [t ein guter Kerl zu sein]
         '. . . because Johann seems a good guy to be'

It is immediately plausible to analyze these cases in terms of the head-government requirement on traces, as is in fact suggested in the references quoted: in (30a) the trace of the raised subject is properly governed by the verb (or by its trace, if the inflected verb moves to Infl in German); in (30b), after extraposition has taken place, the subject trace t is not head-governed and hence ECP is violated. On the other hand, (29b) is well-formed on a par with (29a), as the embedded PRO subject need not (in fact, cannot) be (properly) governed. This analysis implies that proper head government cannot be restored through reconstruction, "undoing" extraposition of the raising complement.

If reconstruction is a property of the LF component, the head-government requirement must apparently be checked at S-structure (possibly at PF; see Aoun, Hornstein, Lightfoot, and Weinberg 1987) on traces created in the syntax. (This does not exclude that it may be checked at LF as well, on traces created in the LF component; see section 2.4 for some relevant evidence.)

Antecedent government differs from head government in that it can be satisfied through reconstruction. This is independently shown by the fact that a preposed phrase can contain an unbound trace of raising, passive or a clitic, provided that the proper-head-government requirement is met. In (31a) and (31b) a VP containing an NP or clitic trace is preposed in Italian; in (31c) an AP containing a Raising trace is pied-piped in English (Longobardi 1985; Browning 1987).

(31) a Messo t in prigione, non sarà t'
       'Put in jail, he will not be'
     b Dato t a Gianni, non l'ho ancora t'
       'Given to Gianni, I not it have yet'
     c How likely [t to win] is John t'

If antecedent government is always compulsory in NP and clitic chains (section 3.4), then it must be possible to restore this relation under reconstruction no matter what technique is adopted for reconstruction (Barss 1986; Cinque, forthcoming). The cases of (31) then pattern on a par with (27a) and contrast with (27b), (28b) and (30b), as the latter involve a head-government violation that cannot be salvaged through reconstruction. The fact that head government and antecedent government must be satisfied before and after reconstruction, respectively, provides clear additional evidence for the postulation of two separate principles, as in conjunctive ECP.

2.3.4   I-to-C Movement in English

A potentially serious problem for our analysis of the limited applicability of Heavy NP Shift is raised by the fact that the interrogative form of a sentence like (14b) is as ill formed as the declarative form. In the interrogative, after the inflected auxiliary has been moved to the head of Comp, the representation should be as in (32), and one would, *a priori*, expect the moved inflection to properly govern the subject trace.

(32)   *[are] [t I intelligent] all the students who can solve this problem?

Why doesn't Subject-Aux inversion improve things? The hypothesis that Subject-Aux inversion is a PF phenomenon, and as such is unable to interfere with an ECP violation, does not seem satisfactory, in the lack of precise assumptions on the nature of PF processes; moreover, Subject-Aux inversion affects various scope phenomena (Liberman 1974; Culicover and Rochemont 1987), an effect that could not be determined by a PF rule; and important differences in the effects of movement to Comp of the inflected verb in English and French can have a principled account if the relevant processes take place in the syntax (Rizzi and Roberts 1989 and references cited there).

A more interesting possibility is that the ill-formedness of (32) is related to the fact that subject-aux inversion does not apply when the subject is *wh*-moved. In both cases, a subject trace immediately preceded by an inflected auxiliary is ill formed:

(33) a *Who did [t see Mary]
     b Who did [Mary see t]

(A sentence corresponding to (33a) is of course possible with emphatic *do* in Infl, a representation that is irrelevant here.) I agree with Koopman (1983, 1984) that this additional subject-object asymmetry should be dealt with through the ECP. But how can these facts be accommodated within our analysis?

A promising first approximation to a satisfactory answer seems to be the following: a head intrinsically inert for government does not acquire the relevant governing capacity if a governing head is moved into it; if C is *per se* inert for government, the fact that it hosts a governing inflected auxiliary in some structures does not turn it into a governor of the appropriate kind (see also Koster 1987). Representations like (32) and (33a) are, then, still ruled out by the ECP.[8]

Let us try to be more specific. It is presumably too strong to assume that the inflection moved to C^0 in subject-Aux inversion structures does not head-govern at all, in view of the fact that the subject still receives nominative case, and PRO is disallowed. A nuanced interpretation is offered by the hypothesis proposed in Rizzi and Roberts 1989 on the derived structure of (root) I-to-C movement. I is substituted into the empty C slot, giving rise to the following configuration:

(34)

$$
\begin{array}{c}
\text{CP} \\
\text{C}^0 \quad \text{C}' \\
\mid \qquad \text{IP} \\
\text{I}^0 \quad \text{NP} \quad \text{I}'
\end{array}
$$

Why shouldn't government by I^0 fulfill the head-government requirement on the subject trace? Our hierarchical definition of proper head government immediately gives the desired result: in (34) C^0, inert for government, does not govern NP; I^0 governs NP, but not within its immediate projection (C′ is not the immediate projection of I^0, and I′ does not contain the subject NP); therefore, the subject trace is not properly head-governed. (The alternative definition in terms of canonical head government would not allow us to obtain the same result in an equally straightforward manner.)

2.3.5 Verb-Second Languages

Comparative considerations become relevant at this point. Structures involving movement of an inflected verbal element to C^0 and movement of the subject to Spec of C, impossible in English, are well formed in German, Dutch, and Scandinavian languages, and other Germanic languages and dialects. For instance, under current assumptions, a simple main declarative clause with subject-initial order has the following representations in German and Danish, with the subject moved to Spec of C and the inflected verb moved to C^0:

(35) a [Johann [hat [t [Maria gesehen] Infl]]]
　　　　'Johann　has　　Maria seen'
　　b [John [har [t Infl [set Marie]]]]
　　　　'John　has　　　　seen Marie'

(See Schwartz and Vikner 1989 for a recent discussion and new evidence supporting this straightforward analysis of the Verb-Second (V-2) phenomenon stemming from Thiersch 1978 and den Besten 1983; see also the different contributions in Haider and Prinzhorn 1986.) Moreover, subject extraction from an embedded clause having undergone V-2 is fully acceptable in German:

(36) Wer hat sie gesagt [t' [ist [t gekommen]]]

How does the subject trace fulfill the proper-head-government requirement in (35) and (36)? The main difference separating these languages from contemporary English is that only the latter has lost productive Verb Second (Subject-Aux Inversion being a construction-specific relic). Suppose that, along the lines of the analysis initiated by den Besten (1983), the defining property of productive V-2 languages is a C^0 intrinsically endowed with appropriate morphosyntactic features (tense features, according to den Besten's original proposal; see Tomaselli 1989 for a recent development of this trend); these features may attract I^0, thus triggering V-2 structures in all root and some embedded tensed clauses, and give C^0 a governing force adequate to license a subject trace in cases like (35) and (36). In a non-V-2 language, such as English, the construction-specific residual case of I-to-C movement is triggered (in a way that remains to be clarified) by a (root) C^0 specified +*wh*—a feature that, contrary to T, does not belong to the class of potential governors and hence does not affect the (lack of) governing capacity of C^0. The fact that within the Germanic family only English disallows I^0-to-C^0 movement across a subject trace is thus related, through the ECP, to the loss of productive V-2, the other major property singling out English among the Germanic languages.[9]

We can now ask a related question: In the Germanic languages with productive V-2, do subject-object asymmetries ever arise in non-V-2 structures, i.e., in embedded tensed sentences in which C^0 is filled by an overt complementizer or by the feature +*wh* in indirect questions? The point is relevant for the proposed analysis of the special status of English (if the other Germanic languages did not manifest subject-object asymmetries at all, it would be less plausible to directly relate the well-formedness of (35) and (36) to V-2), but it also bears on a more fundamental issue: comparative considerations within the Germanic family should give us clear evidence bearing on the choice between the linear and the hierarchical formulation of proper head government. Let us see why.

A clear typological prediction of a definition in terms of canonical government is that *that*-trace effects are a property of SVO languages. Consider the position of Infl in the major language types with respect to word order:

(37) S I V O
      I V S O
      S O V I

In VSO and SOV languages Infl canonically governs the subject, and only in SVO languages is Infl "on the wrong side" of the subject. It is then predicted by the linear definition of head government that a subject trace will be always licensed by Infl in VSO and SOV languages, and only SVO languages will, in general, disallow subject extraction, unless some special device is provided.

On the other hand, the hierarchical approach predicts uniformity (all other things being equal) between the different language types with respect to *that*-trace effects: if a trace must be head-governed within the immediate projection of the head, an inflectional head will never be able to license a subject trace in its specifier, irrespective of linear order. Therefore, according to the hierarchical definition, a subject trace has no privileged status in SOV languages: its governing Infl cannot license it, so if the next potential governor C^0 has the appropriate governing force, it will be licensed; if not, it will not be licensed, and a familiar subject-object asymmetry will arise.

In short, the linear definition predicts that subject-object asymmetries with respect to extraction never arise in SOV languages, while the hierarchical definition predicts that they can arise, depending on the nature of C^0. A scrutiny of the relevant literature on the Germanic languages shows that the hierarchical definition makes the right prediction. Subject-object asymmetries in extraction from *that* clauses have been detected in Dutch varieties sometimes (Perlmutter 1971; Maling and Zaenen 1978) and, more systematically, in German varieties (Marchini 1986; Fanselow 1987, chapter 2 and references quoted there). For instance, Fanselow mentions the following contrast, holding in Northern varieties of German[10]:

(38) a ?Was glaubt Hans, dass Fritz gestohlen hat?
         'What believes Hans that Fritz stolen has?'
      b *Wer glaubt Hans, dass das Auto gestolen hat?
         'Who believes Hans that the car stolen has?'

Moreover, Fanselow reports extraction of a subject from a *wh* island in German to be systematically worse than object extraction. The examples in (39) are adapted from this reference; the diacritics are based on my informants, who find object extraction quite deviant but better than subject extraction (see also Bayer 1989):

(39) a ??Radios habe ich vergessen wie man t repariert
         'Radios have I forgotten how one repairs'
      b *Linguisten habe ich vergessen wie t Radios reparieren
         'Linguists have I forgotten how repair radios'

The general picture thus looks as follows: In V-2 structures all Germanic languages with productive V-2 do not manifest any subject-object asymmetry (irrespective of whether their basic order is OV, as in German and Dutch, or VO, as in Scandinavian); in non-V-2 structures some Germanic varieties manifest subject-object asymmetries (also in OV languages). This is not expected under the linear definition of proper head government, which predicts a uniform lack of subject-object asymmetries in OV, Infl-final languages. The existence of such asymmetries and the fact that the nature of C^0 clearly affects subject extraction also in OV languages thus support the hierarchical definition. The fact that asymmetries are generally absent in V-2 structures, while they tendentially arise in cases of extraction from a *wh* island and may arise (with dialectal variation) in cases of extraction from *that* clauses, strongly suggests that the critical factor is not the position of Infl but the governing nature of Comp, as the hierarchical definition predicts.[11]

This argument thus reinforces the other comparative evidence concerning the nonextractability of the AP Spec (subsection 2.3.2) in supporting the hierarchical definition of head government.[12]

2.3.5 *For* Clauses

A different implication of the proposed analysis is worth exploring in this context. Our explanation of the ill-formedness of (33a) immediately suggests an account of the fact that the subject governed by the prepositional complementizer *for* cannot be moved (Chomsky and Lasnik 1977):

(40) a   I would prefer [for [Bill to win]]
  b   *Who would you prefer [for [t to win]]
  c   *Bill was preferred [for [t to win]]
  d   *I would prefer [for [t to win] the candidate who . . .]

Neither *wh* movement, nor NP movement, nor Heavy NP Shift can affect the subject here. If, taking literally the idea of a prepositional complementizer, we are ready to admit that the structure is that shown in (41), with a preposition-like element inserted under C^0, the analysis proposed for (33a) extends automatically.

(41)

A trace in subject position in (41) would not be properly governed, as the minimal category containing the governor (P) and the governee is not the immediate projection of the governor.

There is another case in which a propositional structure is introduced by a preposition: the absolute *with* construction, in which this preposition selects a small clause, as in (42).

(42) The department is in good shape, with John at its head

But here there is no reason to assume that the whole construction is different from a PP headed by *with* (Van Riemsdijk 1978; Ruwet 1982). The proposed approach to the head-government requirement thus predicts an asymmetry between *for* and *with* with respect to the capacity to license a trace in subject position. As the *with* construction is an adjunct, the prediction is not testable with extraction processes, always excluded on independent grounds, but it is testable with heavy NP Shift of the subject:

(43) a   *I would very much prefer for t to be at its head a prominent
   scientist educated in the U.S.
  b   ?The department is in good shape, with t at its head a
   prominent scientist educated in the U.S.

(43b) is somewhat marginal, but clearly better than (43a). This is now expected: the subject trace is governed by the preposition within its immediate projection, P′; hence, it is properly governed and the ECP is respected.[13, 14]

2.4 Adjuncts

Subject-aux inversion applies when an adjunct is *wh*-moved:

(44) How did [you solve the problem t]

This additional asymmetry between subjects and adjuncts is now expected because the two requirements of the ECP are fulfilled separately in this case: the adjunct trace is properly governed by the verb (or by T^0: see below) and antecedent governed by the *wh* element in the spec of C. The presence of the inflected auxiliary in the head of C does not affect the antecedent-government relation under relativized minimality. In this system the following generalization is not accidental:

(45) a *Who do you think that t came?
     b *Who did t come?

(46) a   How do you think that he came t?
     b   How did he come t?

Here subject traces give rise to *that*-trace effects and do not allow subject-aux inversion, while adjunct traces do not give rise to *that*-trace effects and allow subject-aux inversion. Both differences are derived from the different status of the two types of traces with respect to the head-government requirement, which is fulfilled for the adjunct traces but not for the subject traces in these structures.

Causal and other sentential adverbials also involve subject-aux inversion when *wh*-moved:

(47) Why did John leave

How is the trace of *why* properly head-governed here? If these adverbs are VP-external, the verb is not a candidate. One possibility is that it is governed by some inflectional head. A more radical possibility is that the problem does not arise because there is no clause-internal trace in these cases: sentential adverbs, in order to be properly interpreted, simply require to have the clause they modify in their immediate c-domain, and hence the *wh* version of a sentential adverb can be directly base-generated in Comp (from which it can be moved to a higher Comp in cases of *wh* extraction). This possibility is independently suggested by Longobardi (forthcoming); see also Bromberger 1986.

French provides two arguments in favor of the second conclusion. First of all, whereas other *wh* elements including VP adverbials can be left *in situ*, *pourquoi* (why) cannot (D. Sportiche, personal communication; Aoun 1986):

(48) a   Il a [parlé de quoi]
          'He spoke about what'
     b   Il a [parlé comment]
          'He spoke how'
     c   *?Il a [parlé] pourquoi
          'He spoke why'

The ECP can immediately account for this fact if the assumption is made that no inflectional projection can properly head-govern *pourquoi* in (48c). If this is correct, then at LF, after movement to the spec of C, the traces of *de quoi* and *comment* are properly head-governed by the verb, while the trace of *pourquoi* gives rise to an ECP violation. This of course implies that in (49) no trace of *pourquoi* is left within the clause:

(49) Pourquoi a-t-il parlé
     'Why did he speak'

But why should it be the case that inflectional heads are unable to properly govern a reason adverbial? If adverbials are adjoined to the category they modify, then a sentential adverbial will be adjoined to a sentential projection, either TP or AgrP, under the assumptions of section 2.2. It is then too high to be properly head-governed by T^0. Agr^0 appears to have the special property of being restricted to govern only the element it agrees with (which is, in the general case, its specifier). Thus, traces of sentential adverbials will lack a proper head governor, and will be excluded in general.[15]

The second piece of evidence against local movement to Comp of sentential adverbials is that stylistic inversion is triggered by a complement and a VP adverb, but not by *pourquoi*:

(50) a   De quoi a parlé Jean
          'Of what spoke Jean'
     b   Comment a parlé Jean
          'How spoke Jean'

c *?Pourquoi a parlé Jean
   'Why spoke Jean'

(See de Cornulier 1974 and the note on page 617 of Kayne and Pollock 1978.) If, as Kayne (1986) argues, the possibility of stylistic inversion is somehow parasitic on the presence of a well-formed operator-variable chain, the deviance of (50c) follows: the *wh* sentential adverb that is base-generated in Comp does not bind any variable. Stylistic inversion with *pourquoi* is thus excluded on a par with the cases of other unmoved operators[16]; see (51).

(51) *Je ne sais pas si a parlé Jean
     'I don't know whether spoke Jean'

A somewhat more complex pattern is raised by the possibility of moving adjectival predicates of small clauses. Compare the following examples:

(52) a How intelligent do you consider John t
    b How happy would she make him t
    c How flat did she hammer the metal t

(53) a *How angry did you meet Bill t
    b *How raw did he eat the meat t

(54) How angry did he seem t

(55) *How angry did he telephone t

The fundamental generalization (Chomsky 1986b; Roberts 1988b) appears to be that selected small clausal predicates can be extracted, whether they modify the object, as in (52), or the subject, as in (54), whereas adjunct small clauses cannot be moved, even to the local Comp, whether they are predicated of the object or of the subject (see (53) and (55)).

I would like to explore the possibility that these restrictions are to be derived from the head-government requirement on traces. Let us first consider subject small clauses. Cases like (54) instantiate a selected small clause whose subject undergoes Raising. A more adequate representation would then be the following, in which t' is the NP trace and t is the AP trace:

(56) How angry did he seem [t' t]

Whatever the categorial status of the small clause, we know it must be permeable to external government. Therefore t is properly head-governed from the main verb, on a par with t'. As for (55), if the adjunct small clause must m-command and be m-commanded by its subject (on the motivation of this condition see below), then it is within (the highest) inflectional projection, and the case is reducible to the impossibility of moving a causal adjunct from this position; the proper-head-government requirement could not be satisfied.[17]

Consider now selected small clauses such as those in (52). The small clausal predicate is always properly governed by the verb, and movement is thereby allowed. What about the nonextractability of the adjunct small clauses? Roberts (1988b) relates it to a refinement of Relativized Minimality, which basically amounts to introducing a new class of typical potential antecedent governors for (traces of) elements assigning Theta roles. Here I would like to explore the possibility that it may be derivable from the system as is—more precisely, from our formulation of the head-government requirement on traces. The key question that arises is: What is the structural position of adjunct small clauses predicated of the object, as in (53)? I will maintain the standard assumption that the first projection of a head can contain only lexically selected material; therefore, unselected small clauses cannot be under V'; on the other hand, the small clause cannot be too far from the V', as the strong locality conditions on the subject-predicate relation must be met. As the strongest possible locality condition (mutual c-command, sisterhood) could not be met here because the predicate is outside V' for principled reasons, I will assume that a slightly weaker condition holds on predication: the "subject" and the predicate must be in a relation of mutual m-command. This then implies that the adjunct small clause must be a daughter of VP, outside V' but capable of m-commanding and being m-commanded by the object NP. Selected and unselected small clauses would then differ structurally as follows:

(57)

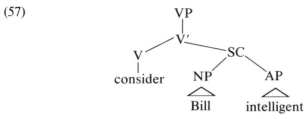

(58)

```
              VP
          ____|_____
        V'                 AP
      __|__               /\
     V     NP            raw
     |    /\
    eat  the meat
```

In (57) the AP can be moved, as its trace is head-governed by V within its immediate projection. In (58) the AP trace could not be properly head-governed (it is not within the immediate projection of V, and it is protected from external head government under minimality; see note 4 to chapter 1); therefore, movement of the adjunct AP is impossible, and the peculiar behavior of adjunct small clauses is explained.[18]

Of course, this solution raises again the issue of VP adverbials: If an adjunct hanging from VP is not movable, as we now have to assume in general, why is it that VP adverbials (e.g., manner adverbials) are locally movable to Comp? In order to answer this question, we must again make crucial use of the more articulated structure of sentential projection in which Agreement and Tense give rise to independent functional projections in that order, the lower immediately dominating the V projection. This more articulated structure gives rise to more possible sites of attachment for the different types of adverbial elements:

(59)

```
              Agr P
          ___/    \___
        NP          Agr'
                  __/   \___
               Agr⁰        TP
                        __/   \___
                      TP        Reason Adv
                      |
                      T'
                   __/  \__
                 T⁰       VP
                       __/  \___
                     VP       Manner Adv
                   __/  \___
                 V'       Adj AP
              __/  \___
            V⁰       SC
                  __/  \__
                NP       AP
```

If VP (Manner) adverbials are (or at least can be) adjoined to VP, then they can be properly head-governed by T^0 across the transparent VP segment; hence, they are movable in general. The option of base-generated VP-adjunction is not available to adjunct AP's predicated of the object, as they must remain included within the VP in order to fulfill the mutual-m-command requirement of the predication relation. Therefore, they are not extractable. Argumental AP's remain properly head-governed by V^0, and hence extractable, as before. As for reason adverbials (as well as all other sentential adverbials), we continue to assume that they are distinct from VP adverbials in that they are adjoined to some functional projection. Whether this is a projection of Agr or of T, their traces will be too high to be properly head-governed by V^0 or T^0, nor will they be properly head-governed by Agr^0 (which is restricted to govern elements coindexed with it) or by C^0 (which is generally inert for government, or otherwise inadequate to fulfill the head-government requirement on an adverb trace when it is turned into a governor for the subject through the technique discussed in section 2.4). Hence, the only possibility of *wh* "movement" for a sentential adverbial will be direct base generation in the Spec of Comp (and the possibility of further extraction from Comp to Comp), with the consequences discussed above.[19]

2.5 Agreement in Comp

Why are the following structures acceptable?

(60) Who do you think [t 0 [t left]]

(61) Who 0 [t left]

Within the framework of assumptions we have adopted in this chapter, only one possibility is left open: something must happen to a null head of Comp when the spec of Comp is filled by a *wh* operator or trace; in such a configuration, the usually inert head of Comp turns into a (proper) head governor. What kind of relation can there be between the two elements, and how can it affect the governing properties of C?

In the traditional theory of Comp, various forms of index percolation or coindexation were stipulated to ensure the desired result in cases of successful *wh* extraction of subjects in different languages (Aoun, Hornstein, and Sportiche 1981; Lasnik and Saito 1984). As was originally pointed out by Adriana Belletti, the analysis of Chomsky 1986b creates the possibility of looking at the relation between a *wh* operator (or trace) and the head of Comp as a particular case of a general pattern: agreement between a specifier and a head. The theory of agreement can be conceived of essentially along the lines which are now generally assumed for the theory of abstract syntactic Case. Both notions involve a structural relation between a head and a maximal projection in a local environment. Such abstract relations play a crucial role in syntactic theory, have visible syntactic effects, and may or may not have a (more or less rich) morphological manifestation. Morphological manifestations are thus generally assumed to offer important indications on the existence and the nature of Case and agreement relations, but they are not assigned the status of criterial conditions for the existence of such relations. We will adhere to these guidelines in the discussion to follow. (See Browning 1987 for the development of a similar line of argument.)

The idea that spec-head agreement in the domain of Comp creates an appropriate head governor for the subject trace can be implemented in the following manner. In English a tensed complementizer can be realized as *that* or Agr:

(62) $C \rightarrow \begin{Bmatrix} \text{that} \\ \text{Agr} \end{Bmatrix}$

We continue to assume that Agr can both be an independent head with its own autonomous inflectional projection (AgrP) and be assigned to another head as a feature (or a set of features). (62) instantiates the latter case. (As Siloni (1989) points out, the complementarity expressed by (62) is strongly reminiscent of the complementarity between the genitive marker and an overt determiner in the English NP, owing to the alternative realization of D^0 as a lexical determiner or as an abstract Agr triggering genitive case, according to Abney (1987).) The two options are in complementary distribution in standard English (but not in some dialects; see below). Moreover, expansion (62) is optional, hence, a tensed C can be expanded as nothing at all. *That* and an unexpanded C are inert for government, while Agr (or any head bearing agreement features) belongs to the class of governors (see definition (13) in chapter 1). In general, an occurrence of Agr must be licensed by coindexation with its specifier; this is perhaps a primitive property of agreement, or a property to be stated through a generalization of the Binding Theory in the sense of Aoun 1985 and Aoun 1986. In our case, this means that if Agr is selected for the head of Comp, it must be coindexed with its specifier; hence, the Spec position must be filled by a *wh* operator or trace. Under these assumptions, (60) and (61) would be more accurately represented as follows:

(63) Who do you think [t Agr [t Infl left]]

(64) Who Agr [t Infl left]

Here the subject trace is properly head-governed by Agr in the head of Comp and antecedent-governed by the specifier of Comp. The structure thus fulfills the ECP. Now consider again the cases we want to exclude:

(65) *Who do you think [t that [t Infl left]]

(66) *Who did [t Infl leave]

In (65) the head of C is inert for government; hence, the ECP is violated. As for (66), we continue to assume, along the lines of Rizzi and Roberts 1989, that movement of the inflected auxiliary to Comp involves substitution for C^0—a process that, under the Recoverability Principle, is possible only if C^0 is radically empty (i.e., no expansion of (62) is chosen). Therefore, the head of C is inert for government, and movement of the inflected auxiliary cannot turn it into a proper governor, as per our previous discussion.[20]

Consider now the following Heavy NP Shift cases:

(67)   *[t are intelligent] all the students who can solve this problem

(68)   *Are [t Infl intelligent] all the students who can solve this problem?

In (67) there is nothing in the spec of C (heavy NP Shift is not a *wh* construction), so Agr in C could not have its coindexing requirement fulfilled and cannot be licensed in this structure. The head-government requirement on the subject trace is not met, and the structure is ruled out by the ECP. (68) is also ruled out by the ECP as before, on a par with (67) and (66).

Sobin (1987) points out that in various regional dialects of American English *that*-trace violations are acceptable. This being the case, whatever principled explanation is adopted for the effect should be flexible enough to adapt to the observed variation. The system proposed here has this property: we can simply admit that in the dialects in question the complementarity expressed by (62) is not found, and *that* can carry Agr. It is also worth noticing that the flexibility of the system is limited: all other things being equal, we do not expect a dialect of English allowing (69).

(69) *This is the student that I wonder [what C [t I bought t]]

Here the spec of C is filled by a *wh* element different from the subject; hence, the Agr option does not help to overcome the lack of a proper head governor for the subject trace. (Remember that the governing properties of Agr appear to be restricted to the elements coindexed with it; an occurrence of Agr in the embedded C of (69), if possible at all, would be coindexed with the object, and hence it could not govern the subject trace.) The rigid exclusion of (69) seems to be in accordance with the results of Sobin's variation study.[21]

A pattern analogous to Sobin's dialectal varieties is reported to exist in Modern Hebrew by Shlonsky (1988). *Wh* extraction of a subject is possible across the declarative complementizer *she* also in structures which do not allow a null pronominal subject, e.g., with present tense:

(70) Mi at ma'mina she-lo ohev salat xacilim?
      'Who you believe that not likes salad eggplants?'

On the other hand, extraction from a *wh* island shows a detectable subject-object asymmetry (see also Doron 1983):

(71) a *Mi ein- ex joda'at 'im mesaret ba-milu'im?
         'Who not you know whether serves in reserves?'
      b   Et mi ein- ex yoda'at 'im ha-milu'im me'aifim?
         'ACC+who not you know whether the reserves tire?'

Thus, one could claim that *she* manifests agreement, on a par with *that* in dialectal English. The case can even be assimilated to standard English, if we follow Shlonsky's analysis more closely. Shlonsky observes that *she* ends up cliticized to the adjacent overt X^0 to its right at PF. He proposes that this cliticization process can take place in the syntax, thus vacating C^0, and making the case similar to subject extraction across a null C^0 in standard English. We can immediately incorporate Shlonsky's solution if we assume that when C^0 is vacated it can be filled by Agr, which agrees with its spec and governs the subject trace as in English. Among other things, this approach has the advantage of eliminating the trace of *she*, which, as is generally the case for traces of downgrading movement, should give rise to an ECP violation. No such device is available in the case of extraction from an indirect question, as the Spec of Comp is already filled and cannot license the appropriate Agr specification.[22]

The plausibility of Spec-head agreement in Comp increases considerably if we look at the variety of strategies that are used to allow *wh* movement of the subject (or other clause-internal constituents) across languages. A number of languages show processes of morphological modifications of Comp when a *wh* element is moved to its Spec. We can take the existence of these processes as evidence that UG offers the resource of agreement in Comp—an observation that, under the usual assumptions of cross-linguistic uniformity, reinforces the view that such processes are generally available. Again, this line of reasoning exactly parallels standard arguments concerning Case Theory. A very clear case of overt agreement in Comp is provided by Kinande, a Bantu language spoken in northeastern Zaire. According to the analysis of Schneider-Zioga (1987), interrogatives systematically involve agreement in class between the *wh* element in the specifier position and the head of Comp:

(72) a IyondI   y0   kambale alangIra
        who (cl.1) that (cl.1) Kambale saw
     b aBahI   Bo   kambale alangIra
        who (cl.2) that (cl.2) Kambale saw
     c EkIhI   ky0   kambale alangIra
        what (cl.7) that (cl.7) Kambale saw
     d EBIhI   By0   kambale alangIra
        what (cl.8) that (cl.8) Kambale saw

This agreement takes place obligatorily with a *wh* element and optionally with a *wh* trace. (On agreement in Comp in the Bantu family, see also Carstens and Kinyalolo 1989.)

   Chung and McCloskey (1987) note that in Modern Irish any clause from which a *wh* element is moved takes a special complementizer, *aL*, replacing the usual complementizer *go*. They interpret this change in the form of C as a visible reflex of the presence of a trace or an operator in the specifier of C. In our terms, the natural further step is to interpret this modification as a reflex of the fact that Spec-head agreement has taken place in the domain of Comp:

(73) An rud aL shil me aL duirt tu aL dheanfa t
     The thing that thought I that said you that you-would-do

   Chung and McCloskey (1987) note that if a complementizer of a sentence from which a *wh* element has been extracted is not changed to *aL*, the sentence is mildly deviant, with the typical flavor of a subjacency violation. It thus appears that in Irish, contrary to Kinande, spec-head agreement with a trace is obligatory: it does not apply in a given Comp in the path between a *wh* operator and its trace only if *wh* movement has skipped that Comp position, thus leaving no trace to agree with and producing a subjacency violation.

   French and West Flemish appear to have very similar Spec-head agreement processes, much more restricted than those of Kinande and

Irish. A significant body of work has been devoted to the rule converting *que* into *qui* in French *wh* constructions:

(74) L'homme que je crois [t qui [t viendra]]
     'The man who I think that will come'

In our terms, this rule simply is the morphological reflex of the application of Spec-head agreement between a trace and the head of Comp. More precisely, *qui* = *que*+*Agr*. The agreement option is much more restricted in French than in the cases discussed above. It occurs only when the subject adjacent to C is extracted. Extraction of an object or of an embedded subject cannot be marked by *qui*:

(75) L'homme que je crois [t que/*qui [Jean connatt t]]
     'The man that I believe that Jean knows'

(76) L'homme que je pense [t que/*qui [Jean croit [t qui [t viendra]]]]
     'The man that I think that John believes that will come'

The same constraint holds of the *da* → *die* rule of West Flemish (Bennis and Haegeman 1984; Haegeman 1983; Haegeman, forthcoming):

(77) Den vent da Pol peinst [t da [Marie t getrokken heet]]
     'The man that Pol thinks that Marie photographed has'

(78) Den vent da Pol peinst [t die [t gekommen ist]]
     'The man that Pol thinks that come is'

Hence, in our terms, Agr in C in French and West Flemish must be identical (coindexed) to Agr in I, whereas there is no such restriction in Irish and Kinande. We can conceptualize this restriction in the following manner. We know that across languages agreement can involve a head and its specifier or a head and its complements (e.g., in languages with object agreement; see Belletti's (1989) analysis of participial clauses in Italian). Both kinds of agreement are attested in the domain of Comp. Spec-Head agreement is instantiated by the Bantu case already discussed. We can interpret some cases of agreeing Comp in various Germanic dialects (Bayer 1984; Bennis and Haegeman 1984; den Besten 1983) as agreement of C^0 with its complement, IP; for example, Bavarian *Wenn-st du kumm-st* (Bayer 1984) can be interpreted as involving C^0 agreeing with IP and hence with IP's head I^0, which in turn agrees with the subject (by transitivity, C^0 also agrees with the subject). We can now look at *qui* and *die* as manifesting a C^0 that simultaneously agrees with its spec and with its complement. The last case can arise only when the local subject is *wh*-moved through the spec of C^0:

(79) [t′ C^0 [t I^0 . . .

Here t′ agrees with C^0, t agrees with I^0, and hence, as t and t′ are identical, by transitivity C^0 agrees with the maximal projection of I^0, its complement IP. Only when this double agreement is realized does C^0 acquire the special form.

Aside from the case of relative clauses (to be discussed in section 2), the special form of the agreeing complementizers involves only cases of extraction from declaratives, not local movement of the subject in questions; in other words, *qui* and *die* are the agreeing forms of $-wh$ C^0. A case that appears to represent the mirror image of the one just discussed is Norwegian *som*. With relatives (in which it is analogous in distribution to English *that*) again put aside, *som* appears only in (embedded) questions when the local subject is moved (Taraldsen 1986):

(80) a Vi vet [hvem *(som) [t snakker med Marit]]
         'We know who that talks with Mary'
     b Vi vet [hvem (*som) [Marit snakker med t]]
         'We know who that Mary talks with'

som does not appear in main questions, as the C^0 position is filled by the inflected verb in V-2 structures; moreover, it does not appear when the embedded subject of a declarative is extracted, as in (78). Thus, *som* and *qui* are alike in that both manifest a C^0 simultaneously agreeing with its complement and its specifier; they differ in that *qui* only manifests a $-wh$ C^0, and *som* only manifests a $+wh$ C^0.

I have argued that a variety of phenomena affecting the form and the syntactic properties of C^0 across languages can be reduced to a unique abstract process: agreement in the domain of Comp. A few simple parameters determine the impressive cross-linguistic variability observed in this domain: agreement of C^0 with its specifier, or with its complement, or with both; restricted to $+wh$ or $-wh$ C^0; optional or obligatory. These parameters are not unique to agreement in Comp: they simply are the specific manifestation in this domain of the dimensions of cross-linguistic variation that the theory of agreement must assume in general.

I have stressed the similarity between French and West Flemish with respect to agreement in Comp. However, the two languages show an interesting difference: in the latter agreement is optional, whereas in the former it is apparently obligatory when possible. Compare (74) and (78) with (81) and (82).

(81)   Den vent da Pol peinst [t da [t gekommen ist]]
        'The man that Pol thinks that come is'

(82)   *L'homme que Jean croit [t que [t est venu]]
        'The man that Pol believes that is come'

Is this difference related to other major differences between the two grammatical systems? A positive answer seems to be possible. French and West Flemish also differ in that the latter, but not the former, is a productive V-2 language; moreover, Haegeman (forthcoming) argues that in general a tensed C^0 has intrinsic governing properties, also in non-V-2 contexts (it assigns nominative case under adjacency to the subject, and bears overt number agreement with the subject). As such, it will be able to properly govern a trace in subject position under the hierarchical definition whether or not C^0 agreement with the spec of Comp takes place. Thus, the hierarchical definition of proper head government allows a principled explanation of the contrast in (81) and (82) by relating the observed difference to a major independent difference between the two languages.[23]

Turning to a different facet of the idea of agreement in Comp, we can exploit its properties in connection with some curious instances of exceptional case assignment. Godard (1985) describes a variety of French in which the following generalization holds: *que → qui* is naturally applicable exactly with the class of verbs which allow the surprising *wh* extraction of the subject of the infinitival complement analyzed by Kayne (1984, chapter 5). That is, the following two options appear to be lexically related in this variety of French:

(83) L'homme que je crois [t qui [t est intelligent]]
     'The man who I believe that is intelligent'

(84) L'homme que je crois [t C [t être intelligent]]
     'The man who I believe to be intelligent'

This state of affairs can be described very naturally within our assumptions: the relevant predicates (epistemic verbs and verbs of saying) select Agr in the embedded Comp, in both tensed and untensed clauses. Thus, a more precise representation of (84) would be the following:

(85) L'homme que je crois [t Agr [t être intelligent]]

The trace in subject position is thus properly head-governed. This hypothesis allows us to solve some traditional problems raised by the analysis of this construction. If a lexical subject stays *in situ*, the structure is ill formed and the only possible unmoved filler of the subject position is PRO:

(86)   *Je crois [[cet homme être intelligent]]
         'I believe this man to be intelligent'

(87)   Je crois [[PRO être intelligent]]
         'I believe to be intelligent = . . .that I am intelligent'

This is the pattern that we would normally expect, given that *croire*, contrary to its English counterpart, is not an exceptional case-making verb, and hence the embedded subject position is protected from government by V and can only be PRO. But if this is correct, how can the *wh* variable survive in a non-Case position in (85)? Kayne's original answer was that the verb Case-marks not the *wh* trace in subject position but the trace in (the Spec of) Comp. Two additional questions were raised by this solution: Why is it that only in this structure is Case assigned to a trace in A' position and not to the variable in A position? Why is this option not available with every infinitival complement—what excludes structures such as (88) and (89)?

(88)   *L'homme que je désire [t O [t gagner]]
         'The man who I desire to win'

(89)   *Who did you try [t O [t to go]]

The analysis proposed above immediately accounts for the two problems: Case can be assigned under government by the selected Agr in Comp to the trace in subject position, so a structure like (85) is not exceptional in this respect. (It could still be the case that the Case feature originates in the main verb and is transmitted under government to Agr in Comp, which then assigns it to the subject trace; see note 24.) The option of Agr in Comp does not help in structures like (86) because no movement is involved and hence there is no Spec of Comp for Agr to be coindexed with; we already had reasons to assume that under such conditions the Agr option is not available (see the analysis of the Heavy NP Shift cases). As for the impossibility of (88) and (89), we know that the option of Agr in Comp is lexically restricted, and there is no reason to expect that surprising pattern to be general. In particular, (88) and (89) are ruled out by the fact that the subject trace is not properly head-governed, hence ECP is violated, and there is no case for the subject trace.

Consider also, in the same vein, the following contrast analyzed by Kayne (1984, chapter 1):

(90) a *I assured you [[John to a be a nice guy]]

       b John, I assure you [t [t to be a nice guy]]

I will assume, following Kayne, that (90a) is ruled out because no case can be assigned to the embedded subject. This may be due to the fact that the main verb is not adjacent. But how could case be assigned in (90b)? Adjacency still is not met by the trace in Comp; moreover, we want Case to end up on the variable in argument position, not on the trace in Comp. The Agr-in-Comp idea provides a solution: If Agr in the embedded Comp can be selected by *assure*, then it will assign case and will properly govern the subject position. Moreover, Agr in Comp is possible only if an appropriate specifier can license it at S-structure. Therefore, (90b) is possible and (90a) is excluded, as desired.[24]

2.6 Strategies of Subject Extraction

The formulation of the ECP that appears to be supported by the empirical evidence reviewed in this chapter has the surprising consequence of excluding in principle *wh* movement of the subject in the general case: a trace must be head-governed; inflection is too low to govern the subject in the appropriate way, C^0 is, in many languages, inert for government but sufficient to block government by a higher governor under Minimality; it then follows that a trace is not allowed to occur in subject position in the general case. This formal constraint, inherent in the structural design of language, obviously clashes with a natural desideratum of effability: from this viewpoint, the optimal system presumably is one that maximizes the possibility of questioning, relativizing, topicalizing, etc. from all the major argument positions. This tension is resolved by the adoption of language-specific formal devices (drawn from the repertory formally allowed by UG and not functionally determined in any simple sense—see the discussion of the *que* → *qui* rule in the preceding section) that allow particular systems to circumvent the general ban against subject traces. In this way we can understand the otherwise quite surprising fact that the properties and restrictions on object extraction are fairly constant across languages, while the possibilities of subject extraction vary considerably, often in bizarre ways (even in closely related languages, such as the Scandinavian languages; see the introduction to Hellan and Christensen 1986). Three major strategies are found to permit subject variables:

• C^0 can be turned into a governor. Agreement in Comp, discussed at length in the preceding section, is the major device used to achieve this result.

• The most radical way to resolve the problem is to eliminate the subject gap through the insertion of a resumptive pronoun; this can be a particular instance of a generalized resumptive strategy, or a specific rule for the subject position (Swedish) or for all the positions not head-governed in the proper way (Vata).

• In languages in which the position of the subject enjoys a certain amount of freedom, extraction of the subject can take place from a position in which the proper-government requirement is fulfilled. This is the fundamental strategy used in Null Subject Languages.

In this section we will review some cases illustrating the second and the third strategy, starting from the selective or generalized use of resumptive pronouns.

Engdahl (1985, p. 8) reports that the use of subject resumptive pronouns is fully grammaticalized in Swedish in structures in which an ECP violation would otherwise arise, e.g., in subject position of indirect questions:

(91) Vilket ord visste ingen hur det / *t stavas?
'Which word knew noone how it is-spelled?'

As (92) (Engdahl 1985, p. 40) illustrates, resumptive pronouns are marginal or impossible in other positions, including the subject positions of embedded clauses with a null C^0, where a trace is allowed (presumably by a mechanism analogous to the corresponding English structure):

(92) Kalle kan jag sla vad om t / *han kommer att klara sig
'Kalle can I bet about t / he is-going-to succeed'

Moreover, Engdahl shows that these resumptive pronouns have the full behavior of syntactic variables, in that they can license parasitic gaps and can cooccur with gaps in other members of coordinate structures in cases of across-the-board extraction.

This state of affairs can be simply interpreted in terms of Chomsky's (1988) minimal-effort guidelines: Swedish has a language-specific rule spelling out a nominative trace as a pronoun; *wh* chains such as the one in (91) are fully assimilated to movement chains with respect to across-the-board extraction and the licensing of parasitic gaps, but no ECP violation arises, as no empty category is involved on the relevant levels of representation. In cases like (92), in which a more general, less marked device is available to avoid an ECP violation, the spellout rule is blocked (see Chomsky's (1988) discussion of *do* support).

Vata appears to generalize the spellout strategy to all positions that are not governed in the appropriate way (Koopman 1984). In particular, the language does not seem to dispose of any device to render C^0 an appropriate governor; hence, the trace spellout is the only option when the subject is *wh*-moved, not only in cases of extraction but also in cases of local movement to the adjacent Spec of Comp. In object position, the spellout of the trace is not required, as the object trace is always governed by the verb; hence, the spellout is also impossible, in accordance with Chomsky's guidelines[25]:

(93) a àló *(ò) le saká la?
    'Who he eat rice WH?'
   b Yi Kòfí le (*mí) la?
    'What Kofi eat it WH?'

Let us now turn to the third subject-extraction strategy. Perlmutter (1971) observed that Null Subject Languages in general do not show subject-object asymmetries in cases of extraction across an overt complementizer. For instance, in Italian subjects are freely extractable across declarative and interrogative complementizers:

(94) a Chi credi che abbia telefonato?
    'Who do you think that has telephoned?'
   b Un uomo che non so se ci potrà aiutare
    'A man that I don't know if will be able to help us'
   c L'uomo che non so che cosa abbia detto
    'The man who I don't know what said'

It was proposed in chapter 4 of Rizzi 1982a that this property is a consequence of free inversion of the subject. The subject can be placed in postverbal position in tensed clauses:

(95) a Credo che abbia telefonato Gianni
    'I think that has telephoned Gianni'
   b Non so se ci potrà aiutare Gianni
    'I don't know if will be able to help us Gianni'

   c Non so che cosa abbia detto Gianni
     'I don't know what has said Gianni'

Extraction can then take place from postverbal position, where the subject trace can be governed in the required manner. The rather complex evidence available in standard Italian for extraction from postverbal position (Rizzi 1982a; Burzio 1986, section 2.5.3) was then corroborated by more straightforward evidence offered by other Null Subject Languages. Jaeggli (1982) and Raposo (1988) showed that a *wh* subject can be left *in situ* in postverbal position but not in preverbal position in Spanish and European Portuguese, respectively. Brandi and Cordin (1981, 1989) and Safir (1985) showed that, in the Northern Italian dialects in which preverbal and postverbal subjects trigger distinct subject clitics under Infl, in cases of subject extraction the clitic that must occur is the one usually cooccurring with a postverbal subject. Kenstowicz (1984) argued that in the Bani Hassan Arabic dialect preverbal and postverbal (*wh*) subjects differ in Case marking, and that if the subject is *wh*-extracted across an overt Comp, it obligatorily manifests the "postverbal" case marking. Raposo (1988) showed that the one environment in which subject inversion is degraded in European Portuguese (in factive sentential complements involving an inflected infinitival (nonauxiliary) verb) is the only environment in which subject extraction is (equally) degraded. The hypothesis of extraction from postverbal position in Null Subject Languages thus seems to be supported by a solid factual basis.

This hypothesis can now be phrased in the following form: the postverbal subject is (or at least can be) adjoined to VP. The representation of (95a) then presumably is, for the relevant part, the following, with an expletive *pro* filling the preverbal subject position:

(97)

art   telefonato   Gianni

The postverbal subject position is properly governed by inflection; hence, a trace is well formed in this position in the case of subject extraction. (In the more articulated structure discussed in section 2.4, the subject would be properly governed by T^0; see Motapanyane 1988 for evidence that T^0 governs and assigns Case to postverbal subjects in Rumanian.)

The diagnostics used in standard Italian (Rizzi 1982a, p. 152) and in the dialects to detect the extraction site of the subject uniformly point to the postverbal position also in cases of *wh* movement in simple clauses. For instance, the dialects in which preverbal and postverbal subjects trigger different kinds of inflectional clitics (and verbal agreement) require the clitic (and the agreement pattern) triggered by postverbal subjects in simple *wh* questions, not only in clauses with unaccusative verbs. The following examples, illustrating the pattern in Fiorentino, are adapted from Brandi and Cordin 1981:

(98) a   Le tu' sorelle l'hanno telefonato (ieri)
          'Your sisters they-telephoned (yesterday)'
     b   Gl'ha telefonato le tu'sorelle
          'It-telephoned your sisters'

(99) a   Quante ragazze gl'ha parlato con te?
          'How many girls it-spoke with you?'
     b   *Quante ragazze l'hanno parlato con te?
          'How many girls they-spoke with you?'

Thus, it appears to be the case that short movement of the subject from spec of IP to spec of CP is barred in standard Italian and in the dialects, the only possibility being movement from the VP-adjoined position. This restriction posed serious problems within the standard approach to the ECP, as the possibility of a subject trace locally antecedent-governed from a trace in Comp would come for free in that system. The current approach looks more promising in this respect, as the licensing of a subject trace always requires a special mechanism. Within this approach, we could simply state the observed facts of standard Italian and the dialects by assuming that the mechanism of Agr in Comp is not available and that one then has to resort to extraction from postverbal position.

It seems desirable to explore the possibility of a more principled account of this exclusion. Consider the following analysis. If lexical heads protect their specifiers from external government (see note 4 to chapter 1), it could be the case that the strong inflection of Italian, responsible for the positive setting of the Null Subject Parameter, counts as lexical and therefore blocks head government of the subject trace from C^0. Short movement of the subject will then be systematically barred in Italian, and movement from the postverbal position will be the only option. See note 27 of Frampton 1989 for a discussion of (the first version of) my proposal, also made independently by Longobardi (1987, note 40) and, for European Portuguese, by Raposo (1988); this proposal also immediately recalls Kayne's (1989) analysis of clitic climbing, according to which a clitic can be extracted from the VP in languages such as Italian because Infl is able to L(exically)-mark the VP, hence turning it into a nonbarrier in the system of Chomsky 1986b.

Jaeggli (1984, note 4) considered and rejected an analysis close to ours of the impossibility of local subject movement in Italian (within a more traditional disjunctive approach to the ECP) on the basis of the following consideration: languages like Italian allow extraction of an adjunct from a tensed clause, as in (100); hence, the strong Infl does not seem to be able to block the required government relation for the adjunct trace in this case.

(100) Come credi [t che [abbiano riparato la macchina t']]
     'How do you believe that they repaired the car'

Jaeggli was then led to conclude that the impossibility of short subject extraction is not due to the ECP. But notice that this objection does not apply to our analysis based on conjunctive ECP, which draws a sharp distinction between subject traces and adjunct traces. In (100) t' is head-governed within the embedded clause (see section 2.4) and antecedent-governed by t. The latter relation is not affected by the intervening strong Infl under Relativized Minimality. (99b) and similar examples of local movement from Spec of I to Spec of C continue to be excluded because the head-government requirement on the subject trace fails: the strong I^0 does not properly govern the subject trace, but protects it from external head government from C^0. The different status of adjunct movement and local movement of the subject is then reduced to the different means of satisfaction of the head-government requirement in the two cases, under conjunctive ECP and Relativized Minimality.[26]

2.7 Relatives and the Doubly Filled Comp Effect

This section is devoted to two separate but interconnected issues:

• the ECP-related subject-object asymmetries arising in relative clauses

• the theoretical status and the proper parametrization of the Doubly Filled Comp Effect.

An outstanding problem for the proposed analysis of the *that*-trace effect is raised by the general acceptability of subject relative clauses introduced by *that*:

(101) the thing that t happened is terrible

One could try to extend the idea of agreement in Comp to this case; that is, (101) could involve an empty operator triggering agreement on the relative complementizer *that* and thus turning it into a governor for the subject trace. But a full assimilation of (101) to cases of extraction from an embedded clause is made problematic by the observation that the pattern is apparently reversed:

(102) a   The thing that [t happened] is terrible
      b   *The thing 0 [t happened] is terrible

(103) a   *What do you believe that [t happened]
      b   What do you believe 0 [t happened]

That, impossible in embedded declaratives whose subject is extracted, not only can but must appear in order to license a subject trace in relatives.

Things are less problematic in French and West Flemish. In these languages the C^0 capable of licensing a subject trace has the same form in cases of subject relatives and subject extraction from a declarative:

(104) La chose qui t est arrivée est terrible
      'The thing that has happened is terrible'

(105) Que crois-tu qui t est arrivé?
      'What do you think that has happened?'

Thus, the special agreeing form of the complementizer is the same in the two cases.

What about English? A partially uniform analysis of (102) and (103) under the agreement-in-Comp idea seems to be possible through the following consideration. Many languages have a special C^0 for relative clauses, distinct from the declarative Comp—for example, Swiss German has *wo* (Bader and Penner 1988; van Riemsdijk 1989); the Scandinavian languages have *som*, also present with a more limited distribution in questions (Taraldsen 1986); Modern Hebrew has *?asher*; Standard Arabic has *?alladhi* (Borer 1984). Thus, Universal Grammar must offer formal resources to differentiate the two kinds of Comp. It could then simply be the case that the agreeing form of the complementizer in standard English is null in declaratives and overt in relatives, whereas the two agreeing complementizers are formally identical in other languages.

I will now try to refine this idea, and to phrase it within the broader context of the general typology and distribution of complementizers.

A preliminary desideratum of any general approach to complementizer types is that it should be able to draw the distinctions observed across languages.

As some languages have special complementizers for relative clauses, we must be able to somehow differentiate the C^0 position of relatives from the homologous position of declaratives and questions. We also want to account for the fact that, whereas many languages—including Modern English—allow the relative complementizer to show up just in case the relative specifier is not filled by an overt *wh* element (as in (106)), other languages allow the cooccurrence of the two elements (for example, in Middle English the equivalent of (106c) was possible (Grimshaw 1975; Keyser 1975)).

(106) a   The thing which I saw
      b   The thing that I saw
      c *The thing which that I saw

As a first approximation to a typology of complementizer types, I would like to introduce the following feature system, providing a partial specification of the different kinds of C^0:

(107) a $\pm wh$
      b $\pm$pred(icative)

A $+wh$ C^0 must cooccur with a $+wh$ operator in its spec at S-structure and LF; a $-wh$ C^0 cannot cooccur with a $+wh$ specifier (in other words, spec-head agreement with respect to this feature is compulsory in the domain of Comp). A $+$pred C^0 must head a CP which is predicated of a "subject of predication"; a $-$pred C^0 heads a clause which cannot be predicated. The $+wh$ specification is compulsory in questions; the $+$pred specification is the distinctive property of relatives; a double negative specification characterizes declaratives. This feature system gives rise to four cases, which are illustrated in (108).

(108) a +*wh* −pred: (I wonder) what 0   [you saw t]
      b +*wh* +pred: The thing which 0   [you saw t]
      c −*wh* +pred: The thing Op   that [you saw t]
      d −*wh* −pred: (I know)   that [you saw it]

In Modern English, *that* is the spellout of −*wh* in tensed environments; thus, cases traditionally treated as manifesting the Doubly Filled Comp effect can simply be ruled out as involving an inconsistent feature specification of Spec and head[27]:

(109) a *What that happened?
      b *The thing which that happened
                    +*wh*   −*wh*

Finally, languages having a special complementizer for relative clauses can be immediately integrated within our current set of assumptions as grammatical systems whose C^0 selection exploits the +pred feature, which singles out relative clauses. Such a special relative complementizer may or may not allow, in turn, the +wh spcification: if it does, it can cooccur with an overt relative pronoun, as is the case for Bavarian *wo* (Bayer 1984); otherwise it cannot, as is the case for Swiss German *wo* (van Riemsdijk 1989).

Constituent questions always involve *wh* operators; moreover, they never involve predication of any sort. They will, then, always fill the slot corresponding to (108a). Headed relatives, on the other hand, are intrinsically characterized by the property of being predicated; they allow *wh* operators, in which case the C^0 will necessarily be +*wh* and hence phonetically null in Modern English (as in (108b)); they also allow null (or deleted) operators, which we will assume not to be specified with respect to the feature ±*wh* (see Dobrovie-Sorin 1988 for an interesting argument that null operators are not specified +*wh*): in such cases (e.g., (108c)), the specifier will be compatible with a −*wh* C^0, and hence *that* will be allowed to occur. Finally, declarative CP's never involve *wh* operators in their spec, they always allow the −*wh* C^0 *that*, and they are not predicative in a sense in which relatives are. *That* can, of course, cooccur with a *wh* trace in its spec in cases like (110).

(110) How do you think [t that [he solved the problem t]]?

This is expected, as *wh* traces are not specified +*wh* (Lasnik and Saito 1984)); hence, nothing prevents them from cooccurring with a −*wh* C^0.

On the basis of this simple typology of complementizer types, we can go back to paradigm (102) and to its striking contrast with (103). First of all we must exclude the ordinary device permitting subject extraction, an Agr specification in a phonetically null Comp which should license the subject trace. Thus, we should rule out a representation such as (111).

(111) *The thing [Op Agr [t happened]] is terrible

Two possible approaches come to mind. It could be that an empty operator is intrinsically incompatible with a local construal with agreement, this perhaps being a consequence of the anaphoric properties of null operators (Aoun and Clark 1985; Contreras 1986), and of the general incompatibility of anaphoric elements with agreement processes (Rizzi 1989).[28] Alternatively, we could assume, with Tellier (1988), that the traditional analysis in terms of deletion of the operator under identity with the head is correct (Kayne 1974), and that on the relevant level of representation the spec of CP is therefore deleted in (111). In this case, it would be reasonable to argue that the deleted specifier lacks syntactic features altogether and thus cannot license an agreement element in (111): no proper governor can then be provided for the subject trace. Whatever approach is adopted for (111), no problem arises when the operator is overt (either because an overt operator is not anaphoric, or because an overt operator has inherent features able to license agreement; in a theory of anaphora such as Burzio's (1989), in which the property of being anaphoric is closely linked to the lack of intrinsic features, the two approaches virtually coincide):

(112) The thing [which Agr [t happened]] is terrible

What about (101)? The standard analysis (Pesetsky 1982a) involved a rule deleting the relative operator in Comp and transferring its index to *that*, thus turning it into an appropriate governor for the subject trace. If the format of this rule is not immediately compatible with the current restrictive assumptions on the available derivational devices, its effects can be achieved in a somewhat different way, formally closer to the proposal of Borer (1984, pp. 136–137).

We need a device turning the overt complementizer into an appropriate governor here. As we now have excluded on principled grounds the possibility that an agreement specification may be licensed by the null (or deleted) operator, it would seem that the agreement idea could not be extended to this case. But there is another possibility to consider: it could be that relative *that* is in an abstract agreement relation not with its A′ Spec but with the head of the relative. This is rather natural: if there is a predication relation involved in relatives, it is legitimate to expect that the "subject of predication" can agree with (the head of) its predicate. In fact, some languages overtly show this pattern. A case in point is standard Arabic. According to Borer's (1984) description, relative clauses in Standard Arabic select a special complementizer *?alladhi ?allati*, agreeing with the head of the relative in grammatical features. Consider this example (Borer 1984, p. 235):

(113) ra?aytu l-fatata ?allati yuridu ?ax-i an yatawwaza-ha
'I saw the girl that + Agr want my brother that marry − her'

That this kind of agreement actually is with the head, and not with a null or deleted operator, is shown by the fact that examples like (113) involve a resumptive strategy of the kind that can freely violate islands and which therefore does not involve any operator movement. It thus appears that Universal Grammar offers the resource of a special +pred C^0 agreeing with the subject of the predication. We may distinguish this sort of agreement from the ordinary spec-head agreement in Comp by using the A/A′ distinction: agreement with the spec of Comp is agreement with an A′ position; agreement with the subject of a predication is agreement with an A position. Pursuing this approach, I will suggest that in English the +pred C^0 carrying A-Agr is spelled out as *that*, in Scandinavian as *som*, in French as *qui*, and so on. The latter two forms cut across the A/A′ distinction, and simply are the agreeing form of the complementizer (either with its spec or with its "subject"). Standard English, on the other hand, distinguishes two forms, zero and *that*, for A′ and A agreement in Comp (on a par with Standard Arabic). Thus, (101) has the following representation:

(114) The thing [____ [that + Agr [t happened]] . . .

In this case, the presence of A-agreement turns the C^0 into an appropriate governor for the subject position, thus permitting a trace to appear.[29]

A principled exclusion of a structure like (115) as an ECP violation may seem too restrictive, as some languages allow subject relatives with a null complementizer.

(115) *The man came is John

Pesetsky (1982a) put forth the conjecture that the possibility of (115) is generally available in Null Subject Languages. This conjecture is corroborated by fifteenth-century Italian, a Null Subject Language freely allowing null complementizers in declaratives and relatives (contrary to modern standard Italian). As Wanner (1981) observes, subject relatives freely admitted null complementizers in fifteenth-century Italian, on a par with object relatives, as in (116) (see also Scorretti (1981)):

(116) Ch'è faccenda ____ tocca a noi
     'For this is a matter (that) concerns us'

(See Wanner 1981, p. 62.) The analysis of this case is straightforward, on the basis of the proposal made in section 2.6 for Null Subject Languages. Fifteenth-century Italian did not need any device turning C^0 into a governor; as a Null Subject Language with free inversion, it allowed movement of the subject to Comp from postverbal position. (116) can thus receive the following representation:

(117) . . . faccenda [Op C^0 [pro I^0 [[tocca a noi] t]]

Irrespective of whether the moved operator is phonetically null or deleted under identity, its trace is properly governed by Inflection; hence, the structure fulfills the ECP.[30]

Chapter 3
Referential Indices and Argument-Adjunct Asymmetries

3.1 The ECP and Theta Government

This chapter concerns the proper formulation of the Empty Category Principle. The fundamental empirical problem that will be addressed is the nature of the argument-adjunct asymmetries that have been extensively discussed in the recent literature. Since James Huang's seminal work, the distinction between arguments and adjuncts has played a fundamental role in the analytic and theoretical work connected to the ECP; however, the exact definition of the boundary separating the two classes of entities and the way to integrate the distinction within the theory are still quite controversial. I would like to show that the asymmetries are amenable to a straightforward analysis if we assume a very natural restriction on the possible utilization of referential indices as "bookkeeping devices" to keep track of dependencies created by the application of movement rules. This restriction will also permit a radical simplification of the ECP.

Let us start by reviewing certain issues already discussed in the preceding chapters from a slightly different angle.

The following paradigms illustrate some of the basic effects of the ECP. The first example of each triple is a case of subject extraction, the second illustrates object extraction, and the third adjunct extraction (extraction of an adverbial element). The first paradigm concerns extraction from an indirect question. The second concerns extraction from an embedded declarative introduced by an overt complementizer. The third and fourth paradigms illustrate the corresponding cases in Italian, a language that allows phonetically null pronominal subjects in tensed clauses (a Null Subject Language):

(1) a *Which student do you wonder [how [t could solve the
        problem t]]
    b ?Which problem do you wonder [how [PRO to solve t t]]
    c *How do you wonder [which problem [PRO to solve t t]]

(2) a *Which student do you think [t that [t could solve the
        problem]]
    b Which problem do you think [t that [Bill could solve t]]
    c How do you think [t that [Bill could solve the problem t]]

(3) a ?Che studente non sai [come [potrà risolvere il problema t t]]
        'Which student don't you know how could solve the
        problem'
    b ?Che problema non sai [come [potremo risolvere t t]]
        'Which problem don't you know how we could solve'
    c *Come non sai [che problema [potremo risolvere t t]]
        'How don't you know which problem we could solve'

(4) a Che studente credi [t che [potrà risolvere il problema t]]
        'Which student do you think that could solve the problem'
    b Che problema credi [t che [potremo risolvere t]]
        'Which problem do you think that we could solve'
    c Come credi [t che [potremo risolvere il problema t]]
        'How do you think that we could solve the problem'

Let me comment on the different paradigms analytically. (1a)–(1b) is
a classical subject-object asymmetry: a subject cannot be extracted
from an indirect question (*wh* island), whereas object extraction is
marginally acceptable.[1] All the versions of the ECP proposed since
Chomsky's Pisa lectures have tried to capture this sort of asymmetry
in the following way: (1a) violates the ECP, a strong principle; (1b)
does not, and its mild deviance is attributed to the violation of a weaker
principle, Subjacency. A few years ago, James Huang noticed that
extraction of an adjunct, as in (1c), gives rise to a violation as severe
as subject extraction. Huang (1982) made the influential proposal that
the two cases should be treated on a par, as ECP violations. Various
formulations of the ECP proposed in the mid-1980s tried to capture
this apparent symmetry between subjects and adjuncts.

    Still, there are reasons to believe that this analogy is partial, at best.
A simple inspection of the other paradigms suggests a different, more
complex picture. First of all, in cases of extraction from declaratives
with an overt complementizer, adjunct extraction is possible, and

patterns with object extraction, as opposed to subject extraction (see (2) above). Second, in cases of extraction from *wh* islands in a Null Subject Language like Italian, subject extraction is possible on a par with object extraction (the marginality of (3a) and (3b) disappears if the extracted element is a relative pronoun (Rizzi 1982, chapter 2); on the postverbal position of the subject trace see section 2.6 and below), whereas adjunct extraction remains impossible (see (3c)). Paradigm (4) illustrates the different types of extraction from a *that* clause in a Null Subject Language; here the three cases are possible. Particularly significant in the present context are (2) and (3), which manifest a double dissociation between subject and adjunct extraction. This casts serious doubts on the validity of the generalization suggested by (1). Moreover, a single theoretical statement does not seem to capture this articulated picture: there are too many distinctions to be drawn. The theoretical path that we provisionally adopted in chapter 2 is the conjunctive formulation of the ECP. This principle is now assumed to consist of two separate clauses which must be independently fulfilled:

(5) **ECP:** A nonpronominal empty category must be
    (i) properly head-governed (Formal licensing)
    (ii) Theta-governed, or antecedent-governed (Identification)

Proper head government is government by a head within its immediate projection. Theta government is government by a theta assigner (e.g., government of the object by a theta-assigning verb), and antecedent government is government by an antecedent (an element that governs and binds the governee). See sections 1.3 and 2.1 (and appendix 2 of chapter 1) for the formal definitions.

We can now see how this system properly accounts for the paradigms in (1)–(4). In (1a) the subject trace is not properly head-governed. It is head-governed by Infl, but not within its immediate projection, I'. The formal licensing component of the ECP is thus violated. The identification component is also violated: the governor of the subject trace, Infl, is not a Theta assigner (at least, not a Theta assigner for the subject); hence, the subject trace is not Theta-governed; it is not antecedent-governed either, because its antecedent (the *wh* phrase *which student*) is too far away to govern it, under Relativized Minimality.

The structure is then ruled out as a (double) violation of the ECP module. On the other hand, (1b) is ruled in, as far as the ECP is concerned. Here we have to take into account two traces. Consider first the object trace: it is properly head-govened by the verb; moreover, it is theta-governed by the verb; hence both parts of the ECP are met. As for the trace of *how*, the latter being a VP adverbial, it is properly head-governed by the verb (or by T^0, given the refinement in section 2.4), and the formal licensing part is thus met. The adjunct trace is not theta-governed, but it is antecedent-governed by *how* in the local Comp, so that both components of the ECP are met. The mild deviance of the example is attributed to a Subjacency violation, given an appropriate counting of Subjacency barriers (Chomsky 1986b).

Now consider (1c). The object trace passes the ECP test, but the adjunct trace does not. It meets the proper-head-government requirement but not the identification requirement. The adjunct trace is not theta-governed, nor is it antecendent-governed, its antecedent *how* being too far away. The structure is thus ruled out by the ECP module. Within this account, the ill-formedness of (1a) and (1b) still receives a uniform account through the ECP, but the parallelism is partial: (1a) violates both clauses of the ECP, whereas (1c) violates only the identification requirement.

In (2a), the subject trace meets the identification requirement, being antecedent-governed by the trace in Comp (at least in the system of Relativized Minimality), but it fails to meet the formal licensing requirement: it is head-governed by Infl, but not properly. In (2b) both the formal licensing requirement and the identification requirement on the object trace are met by the verb, which properly head-governs and theta-governs it. Moreover, there is no subjacency violation, and the structure is fully acceptable. In (2c) the adjunct variable is properly head-governed by the verb (or T^0); moreover, it is antecedent-governed by the trace in Comp; in turn, the trace in Comp is properly head-governed by the main verb and antecedent-governed by the operator in the main Comp. The two requirements of the ECP are thus met separately in this case.

Why is it that subject extraction is systematically possible from *wh* islands and across overt complementizers in languages like Italian? In section 2.6 it was proposed that this property is related to the fact that in such languages the subject can be placed in VP-final position—that is, alongside (6a) we have (6b), where the preverbal subject position is filled by the phonetically null expletive pronominal *pro*:

(6) a [Un mio studente] [ha] [risolto il problema]
       'A student of mine has solved the problem'
    b *pro* [ha] [risolto il problema] [un mio studente]
       'Has solved the problem a student of mine'

It is, then, natural to analyze cases such as (3a) and (4a) as involving movement of the subject from postverbal position. The subject trace therefore is properly head-governed by Infl here (by T^0, under the split-Infl hypothesis), and the first requirement of the ECP is met. How is the identification requirement fulfilled? We can provisionally assume that the subject trace right-adjacent to the VP is Theta-governed by V or VP (we will come back to this point later on). (3b) and (3c), and (4b) and (4c), are analyzed in the same way as the corresponding cases in English.

3.2 Against Theta Government

The approach to the ECP presented in the preceding section achieves remarkable descriptive and explanatory success. It treats in a natural and minimal way the various argument-adjunct asymmetries, making unnecessary a number of auxiliary assumptions required by other approaches—in particular, the assumption that the ECP applies at distinct levels for arguments and adjuncts (as in the influential trend initiated by Lasnik and Saito 1984). Moreover, it successfully deals with the major cross-linguistic variation attested in this domain.

Still, there are good reasons to doubt the overall correctness of this approach. There are, first of all, fairly obvious conceptual arguments against the form of the ECP given in (5). Theta government is in most cases (perhaps in all cases, depending on the analysis of (3a)) a kind of head government, so both clauses of the ECP require some sort of head government. One should wonder why. There appears to be a disturbing conceptual redundancy in the system. A second problematic property has to do with the disjunctive formulation of the second clause of the ECP. Disjunctive statements are intrinsically unsatisfactory. Admitting a disjunctive formulation amounts to admitting that the nature of a generalization is not understood: if I write a principle as saying that either property A or property B must be fulfilled, I am implicitly admitting that I do not understand the nature of the formal or functional equivalence holding between A and B. Of course a disjunctive formulation can turn out to be extremely productive, and even illuminating at certain stages of the comprehension of an issue (the whole history of the ECP is a good case in point), but the desideratum of avoiding disjunctions is an important one, even in the face of significant descriptive success.

Theta government is at the intersection of the two conceptual problems. It is, then, reasonable to single this notion out for further scrutiny. One possible approach would be to keep the principle essentially as it is and try to do away with the explicit reference to Theta government by formally unifying it with antecedent government, as in Stowell 1981. I would like to develop a different approach, departing more radically from familiar formulations of the principle. Let us first of all take into account some empirical arguments against Theta government.

Consider first lexically selected adverbials. A verb like *se comporter* (to behave) in French obligatorily selects a manner adverbial and optionally selects an argumental comitative complement:

(7) Jean se comporte *(bien) avec les amis
    'Jean behaves (well) with friends'

If we take seriously the spirit of the program of reducing categorial selection to semantic selection (Grimshaw 1979; Pesetsky 1982b; Chomsky 1986a) and we make the minimal assumption that semantic selection is expressed by the thematic (theta) grid in Stowell's (1981) sense, the inescapable conclusion is that the adverbial is mentioned in the theta grid of the verb; there is no other way to express lexical selection within this restrictive program. But then, if the adverbial is theta-marked, it is also theta-governed by the verb; therefore, a theory of the ECP like the one described in section 3.1 would predict it to behave on a par with arguments with respect to extraction—in particular, to be freely extractable from *wh* islands. This prediction is incorrect: lexically selected adverbials behave on a par with nonselected adverbials, (1c). In the case in point, there is a sharp contrast between extraction of the argument and extraction of the adverbial complement of *se comporter* from a *wh* island:

(8) a ?Avec qui ne sais-tu pas [comment [PRO te comporter t t]]
       'With whom don't you now how to behave'
    b *Comment ne sais-tu pas [avec qui [PRO te comporter t t]]
       'How don't you know with whom to behave'

This is not expected given the theory of section 3.1, under reasonably restrictive assumptions on the nature of lexical selection. (Things are somewhat blurred in English by the idiomatic absolute use of *behave* meaning *behave well*; if proper abstraction is made from this case, the argument can be immediately reproduced.)

The same kind of argument is provided by the behavior of lexically selected measure phrases. The case can be illustrated by ambiguous verbs like *weigh*. There is an agentive *weigh*, taking a direct object, and a stative *weigh*, selecting a measure phrase:

(9) a John weighed apples
    b John weighed 200 lbs

Both types of complements can be questioned, at a colloquial level, through the *wh* element *what*. The following question remains ambiguous:

(10) What did John weigh t ?

But if *what* is extracted from a *wh* island, only the agentive reading survives. The marginal question (11) can be properly answered "Apples", not "200 lbs", even in contexts that would make the stative interpretation pragmatically plausible.

(11) ? What did John wonder how to weigh t?

(This observation and this example are due to David Feldman; the same argument is discussed in Koopman and Sportiche 1988.) In general, lexically selected measure phrases pattern on a par with unselected measure phrases in that they cannot be extracted from *wh* islands. This is not expected under the version of the ECP presented in section 3.1, given the theory of lexical representations we have adopted. According to this theory, the two verbs *weigh* presumably differ only in their theta grids, as follows:

(12) a ⟨agent, patient⟩
     b ⟨theme, measure⟩

Both kinds of complements are theta-marked and hence theta-governed; therefore, they should be equally extractable from *wh* islands, contrary to fact.

A similar but independent argument is provided by the behavior of certain idiomatic expressions. It is well known that the nominal parts of some idioms can be *wh*-moved, on a par with the compositional material:

(13) a What headway do you think [t [you can make t on this project]] ?

    b What project do you think [t [you can make headway on t]] ?

But extraction from a *wh* island is significantly more deviant for the idiom chunk:

(14) a *What headway do you wonder [how [PRO to make t on this project]] ?

    b ?What project do you wonder [how [PRO to make headway on t]]

Since this effect has not been described so far (but see Cinque's (1984) discussion on the nonextractability of idiom chunks from stronger islands), it is worthwhile to mention some more cases. The nominal part of the Italian idiom *trarre partito da X* (take advantage of X) can be relativized, but cannot be extracted from an indirect question, in clear contrast with the compositional PP:

(15) a Il partito che penso di trarre dalla situazione è il seguente
       'The advantage that I intend to take of the situation is the following'

    b *Il partito che non so come trarre dalla situazione è il seguente
       'The advantage that I don't know how to take of the situation is the following'

    c La situazione da cui non so come trarre partito è la seguente
       'The situation of which I don't know how to take advantage is the following'

The same effect is shown by the minimal contrast, in Italian, between the compositional expression *prestare i soldi* (to lend money) and the idiomatic expression *prestare attenzione* (to lend attention = to pay attention). In both cases the nominal part can be relativized, but only in the first case is extraction from a *wh* island possible:

(16) a I soldi che ho deciso di prestare a Gianni sono molti
       'The money that I decided to lend to Gianni is a lot'

    b L'attenzione che ho deciso di prestare a Gianni è poca
       'The attention that I decided to lend to Gianni is few'

   c I soldi che non ho ancora deciso a chi prestare sono molti
      'The money that I haven't decided yet to whom to lend is a
      lot'
   d *L'attenzione che non ho ancora deciso a chi prestare è poca
      'The attention that I haven't decided yet to whom to lend is
      few'

Another minimal pair is provided in Italian by *dare X a Y* (to give X
to Y) and *dare credito a Y* (to give credit to Y = to put credit/trust in
Y):[2]

(17) a Che libro pensi di poter dare a Gianni?
        'What book do you think you can give to Gianni?'
     b Che credito pensi di poter dare a Gianni?
        'What credit do you think you can put in Gianni?'
     c ?Che libro non sai a chi dare?
        'What book do you not know to whom to give?'
     d *Che credito non sai a chi dare?
        'What credit don't you know in whom to put?'

According to the restrictive version of the Projection Principle argued
for on page 37 of Chomsky 1981, nominal parts of idioms must receive
a special, quasi-argumental theta role from the verb. Therefore they
are theta-governed; hence the version of the ECP referring to theta
government incorrectly predicts extractability from *wh* islands for
nominal idiom chunks.

   In conclusion: Lexically selected adverbials and measure phrases,
as well as nominal parts of idioms, are theta-marked and theta-governed, under reasonable restrictive assumptions on the nature of lexical representations and on the Projection Principle. A theory of the
ECP based on the notion of theta government would then predict that
such elements should pattern with other lexically selected arguments
in the relevant respects. The prediction is incorrect. These elements
strongly disallow extractions from *wh* islands, on a par with non-
lexically-selected adverbials and other adjuncts.

3.3 The Status of Subject Extraction

A different kind of empirical evidence against a formulation of the
ECP in terms of theta government is provided by long-distance subject
extraction. Concerning extraction of subjects in non–Null Subject lan-

guages, the approach presented in section 3.1 makes a clear prediction: no matter what the depth of the extraction site is, extraction from a *wh* island should be on a par for subjects and adjuncts. Neither kind of trace is theta-governed. They should be antecedent-governed, but if extraction takes place from a *wh* island a required antecedent-government relation necessarily fails to exist, so an ECP violation should arise. The parallelism seems indeed to exist in simple cases of extraction such as (1) and (18), as we have seen. The problem for the theta-government approach is that the subject-adjunct parallelism tends to disappear if we take into account more complex structures obtained by adding one level of embedding. Consider a structure like (19), in which a declarative is embedded within an indirect question, and compare the three kinds of extraction:

(18) a *Who do you wonder whether t can help us ?
      b ??Who do you wonder whether we can help t ?
      c *How do you wonder whether we can help Bill t ?

(19) a ?*Who do you wonder whether we believe t can help us?
      b ??Who do you wonder whether we believe we can help t?
      c *How do you wonder whether we believe we can help
         Bill t ?

Speakers often find structures like (19a) somewhat worse than (19b), but the contrast does not seem to be as sharp as typical contrasts induced by the ECP. This is what Pesetsky (1984) calls a "surprising subject-object asymmetry." We agree with him that the ECP is not responsible for this kind of contrast. (See also the thorough discussion in Browning 1987, where the same conclusion is reached.) On the other hand, adding one level of embedding does not improve things for adjunct extraction: (18c) and (19c) are generally judged on a par, and it appears fully legitimate to give a common explanation to both cases through the ECP. What is unexpected under the theory of section 3.1 is the subtle but systematic lack of parallelism between subjects and adjuncts.[3]

Let us have a closer look at the relevant cases. (19a)–(19c) are more accurately represented as follows:

(20) a Who do you wonder [whether [we believe [(t′) [t can help
         us]]]]
      b Who do you wonder [whether [we believe [(t′) [we can help
         t]]]]

c How do you wonder [whether [we believe [(t′) [we can help
   Bill t]]]]

I will assume, following Pesetsky 1982b, that leaving a trace when
movement takes place is not obligatory *per se* (even though independent principles may enforce the presence of a trace). This optionality
is reflected by the fact that the trace in Comp (t′) is parenthesized in
the preceding structures. Now consider (20c). If t′ is not present, t
violates the identification clause of the ECP: it is not theta-governed,
nor is it antecedent-governed. On the other hand, if t′ is present in
(20c) then t is well formed: it is properly head-governed by the verb
(or by T^0) and antecedent-governed by t′. Thus, the offending trace
must be t′: in fact, it is properly head-governed by the higher verb,
but it is not theta-governed or antecedent-governed, whence the violation. In conclusion: no well-formed representation is associated with
(19c). In (20b), t is properly head-governed and theta-governed by the
verb, and therefore the ECP is satisfied; if t′ is not present, the
structure is well formed as far as the ECP is concerned. The other *a
priori* possible representation of (19b)—the one in which t′ is present—
violates the ECP as in the preceding case, but the crucial fact is that
one well-formed representation (modulo subjacency) can be associated
with (19b).

Now consider (20a). If t′ is not present, t will violate the identification requirement of the ECP, being neither theta-governed nor antecedent-governed. It will also violate the formal-licensing requirement.
If t′ is present, t is antecedent-governed by it. (Moreover, formal
licensing for t is fulfilled through agreement in Comp, or whatever
technique makes short movement of the subject possible; see section
2.5.) But then t′ violates the identification clause of the ECP, and no
well-formed representation is assigned to (19a); the case is thus treated
exactly on a par with (20c) as opposed to (20b). As we have seen, this
is not the partitioning that seems to emerge from the judgments of
relative acceptability, which, if anything, would tend to assimilate
subject and object extraction in these cases. Again, the source of the
problem seems to reside in the uniform status assigned by the theta-
government approach to subjects and adjuncts.[4]

This argument against theta government is reinforced by the essentially parallel behavior of subjects and objects as opposed to adjuncts
in the environment of negative operators. Ross (1983) noticed that
negative elements induce familiar object-adjunct asymmetries:

(21) 1   Who do you think we can help t ?
     b   Why do you think we can help him t ?
(22) a   Who don't you think we can help t ?
     b   *Why don't you think [t′ [we can help him]] ?

It was argued in the first chapter that the impossibility of (22b) in the intended reading (with lower construal of *why*) is excluded by the ECP; in essence, the intervening negative element blocks the required antecedent-government relation for t′. The approach presented in section 3.1 correctly predicts that no problem arises when a direct object is extracted from the scope of negation, as in (22a): t is theta-governed, hence the identification requirement is locally fulfilled, and the representation of (22a) in which no trace is left in Comp is well formed. But this approach incorrectly predicts subject extraction to be on a par with adjunct extraction. A relevant case would be the following:

(23) (?)Who don't you think [(t′) [t can help us]]

If t′ is not present, t should violate the formal-licensing clause of the ECP in the usual manner; if t′ is present, it should violate the identification requirement of the ECP because of the blocking effect of negation on antecedent government. The subject case would then be predicted to be on a par with the adjunct case. But this clearly is incorrect: speakers find at most a slight degradation with respect to object extraction (this is what the parenthesized question mark is meant to suggest), and generally agree that the main dividing line is to be drawn between (22b) and (23)-(22a). An approach based on theta government seems to be intrinsically unable to deal with these cases of argument-adjunct asymmetry in which subjects and objects tend to pattern together, if compared with adjunct extraction. Later on we will return to the "surprising" weaker asymmetry between subject extraction and object extraction.

3.4   A-Chains

A different kind of evidence against theta government, already discussed in the literature, is provided by the locality conditions on A chains (passive and raising). Here I will simply reproduce the argument of Chomsky 1986b. Although distant control from a nonadjacent clause is possible (SuperEqui), long-distance Raising (SuperRaising) is not:

(24)   John thinks [that it is difficult [PRO to shave himself in public]]

(25)   *John seems [that it is likely [t to shave himself in public]]

(Were (25) acceptable, it would have the perfectly sensible interpretation of "It seems that it is likely that John will shave himself in public".) Subjacency and the theory of binding do not seem to properly characterize the strong deviance of (25). Chomsky (1986b) observes that it appears to have the status of an ECP violation. In fact the version of the ECP given in section 3.1 above would seem to achieve the desired result: the subject trace is not theta-governed; it should be antecedent-governed, but the antecedent is too far away in (25); an ECP violation is thus produced. The problem is that this approach cannot capture the fact that passive at a distance is just as impossible as long-distance raising: passivization of (26a) must be local as in (26b), and cannot skip the closest subject as in (26c):

(26) a   It seems that someone told Bill that . . .
     b   It seems that Bill was told t that . . .
     c   *Bill seems that it was told t that . . .

In (26c) the trace in object position is theta-governed by the verb, so the version of the ECP defined in terms of this notion cannot enforce antecedent government here. This approach is, then, unable to give a uniform account of the impossibility of SuperRaising and SuperPassive under the ECP.

A parallel argument can be constructed on the basis of Kayne's (1989) analysis of cliticization in Romance languages. Kayne argues that the clause-boundedness of cliticization is best accounted for by the ECP; for example, the clitic trace is antecedent-governed in (27a) but not in (27b), whence the ill-formedness of the latter:

(27) a   Jean essaie [de le faire t]
          'Jean tries to do it'
     b   *Jean l'essaie [de faire t]
          'Jean tries to do it'

Again, this analysis requires that theta government is not an independent way to fulfill the identification requirement of the ECP. If it was, antecedent government could not be enforced for clitic traces, which in the general case are theta-marked by the governing verb. (This argument holds only if clitic traces are NP's, not N^0's.)

In conclusion: Various considerations have lead us to single out theta government as the source of important conceptual and empirical inadequacies of the ECP, in the version adopted so far. The remainder of this chapter will be devoted to a revision of our current assumptions which will take these problems into account. In order to do that, it is necessary to go back to the many asymmetries noticed so far in extraction processes and try to adequately state the fundamental generalization that emerges.

3.5   On Restricting the Use of Referential Indices

Among the many proposals that can be found in the recent literature, the concise characterization of the fundamental generalization that fits the facts discussed best is the one put forth, for very different reasons and in somewhat different terms, by Joseph Aoun and Guglielmo Cinque: referential elements are (marginally) extractable from islands, nonreferential elements are not.[5]

On preliminary scrutiny, this informal characterization looks sufficiently promising to invite us to inquire further. Consider the asymmetries discussed in section 3.2. Whatever precise definition of "referential" we will end up adopting, it is intuitively plausible that compositional complements should turn out to be referential in a sense in which nominal parts of idioms (*headway, credito*, etc.) are not; similarly, it makes intuitive sense to say that the direct object of agentive *weigh* and the comitative complement of *behave* are referential whereas the measure phrase selected by stative *weigh* and the manner adverbial selected by *behave* are not, and so forth.

My proposal is that the required notion of "referentiality" should be made precise in terms of thematic theory; this is so partly for empirical reasons to be discussed below, and partly because thematic theory already possesses the necessary concepts, and no further elaboration is to be introduced. Thus, if the proposal to be developed eliminates theta government from the ECP module, it still assumes that Theta Theory plays a crucial role in determining the possible occurrence of traces.

The first thing we need is a distinction between two types of theta roles. We continue to assume that all selected elements are theta-marked. Even so, there is a clear distinction to be drawn. Some selected elements refer to participants in the event described by the verb (John, apples, books, etc.); other selected elements do not refer to participants but rather qualify the event (compositionally (measure, manner, etc.) or idiosyncratically (idiom chunks)). This split corresponds, in essence, to Chomsky's (1981, p. 325) distinction between *arguments* (referential expressions potentially referring to participants in the event) and *quasi-arguments* (expressions that receive a theta role but do not refer to a participant, such as the subjects of atmospheric predicates and the nominal parts of idioms). We can thus distinguish argumental or referential theta roles (agent, theme, patient, experiencer, goal, etc.) and quasi-argumental, nonreferential theta roles (manner, measure, atmospheric role, idiosyncratic role in idioms, etc.).

Let us then restate the Aoun-Cinque generalization in terms of Chomsky's split: only elements assigned a referential theta role can be extracted from a *wh* island; everything else (non-theta-marked elements and elements receiving a nonreferential theta role) cannot. What is the theoretical status of this generalization? Cinque's original system is specifically designed to deal with stronger islands (adverbial islands and complex NP's), so that it is not directly applicable to our *wh*-island cases; moreover, our system of assumptions is technically incompatible with Aoun's Generalized Binding approach (even though close to it in various respects). I would like to propose a different, quite straightforward approach, capitalizing on the idea that the term "referential index" should be taken seriously and literally for what it means. The use of referential indices should then be restricted to cases made legitimate by the following principle:

(28) A referential index must be licensed by a referential theta role.

That is to say, a referential index is legitimate on a given linguistic representation only if it is associated to a referential theta role. For concreteness, we can mechanically interpret (28) essentially along the lines of the passage in Chomsky 1965 in which referential indices were first introduced[6]: Suppose that every position receiving a referential theta role is assigned a referential index at D-structure, under (28). The content of this position, if moved, can carry its index along. No other position can carry a referential index, under (28). We continue to assume that the binding relation is defined in terms of the notion of referential index.

(29) X binds Y iff

   (i) X c-commands Y

   (ii) X and Y have the same referential index.

The net effect of (28), then, is to restrict binding relations to elements associated to referential theta roles, much in the spirit of the original approach. We claim that this restriction subsumes the essential effect of the identification clause of the ECP and properly captures the fundamental argument-adjunct asymmetries. We can thus simplify the ECP by reducing it to the former formal licensing requirement:

(30) **ECP:** A nonpronominal empty category must be properly head-governed.

We now are ready to see how the system works, for a first approximation. Principle (28) determines a split within A' dependencies which is visualized in the following structures:

(31) a Who$_k$ did you see t$_k$?

   b How did you behave t ?

In (31a) the operator is connected to its variable through binding, as usual. The index k is licensed by the referential theta role that *see* assigns to its object, and can be legitimately used to express the A' dependency. On the contrary, no indexation is legitimate in the case of (31b) under (28), as no referential theta role is involved. Thus, the A' dependency cannot be expressed through binding. Still, for the structure to be interpretable the operator must be somehow connected to its variable. The system must then resort to some other connecting device. Now, if we look through the modular structure of the theory searching for devices available for establishing interactive connections between positions, we find only two major candidates, the theoretical prominence of which is so obvious that they are often used to refer to the whole framework: binding, used by Binding Theory and Control Theory, and government, used by Case theory, Binding Theory, and the licensing modules of the various types of null elements. Binding being unavailable in (31b), the system must resort to government to connect operator and variable.[7]

Of course, a fundamental difference between the two devices is that binding can hold at an arbitrary distance, whereas government is intrinsically local. There is, then, an essential asymmetry between the two modes of connection. This is the source of the observed asymmetries. Let us reconsider the basic paradigms (1) and (3), repeated here for ease of reference:

(32) a *Which student do you wonder [how [t could solve the problem t]]

b ?Which problem do you wonder [how [PRO to solve t t]]

c *How do you wonder [which problem [PRO to solve t t]]

(33) a ?Che studente non sai [come [potrà risolvere il problema t t]]
'Which student don't you know how could solve the problem'

b ?Che problema non sai [come [potremo risolvere t t]]
'Which problem don't you know how we could solve'

c *Come non sai [che problema [potremo risolvere t t]]
'How don't you know which problem we could solve'

(32a) violates the ECP, now reduced to (30), because the subject trace is not properly governed. In (32b) there are two connections to take into account. The object trace can bear an index under (28), so that it can be connected to its operator over a long distance through binding; the adjunct trace cannot bear an index, but its operator is close enough for government to hold; both connections are thus properly established, and the sentence gives rise to only a mild subjacency violation. On the other hand, (32c) is ill formed: the object trace does not raise any problem, but the adjunct trace does; it cannot be connected to its operator through binding (because indexation is not legitimate in this case) or through government (because the operator is too far away). The connection cannot be established; hence, the sentence is ruled out as uninterpretable. All the basic contrasts discussed in section 3.3 ((8a)-(8b), the two interpretations of (11), (14a)-(14b), (15), etc.) can be analyzed in a similar manner. Examples (33b) and (33c) are dealt with on a par with (32b) and (32c). On the other hand, (33a) is well formed because the subject is extracted from a position which is properly governed by Infl; the ECP (30) is thus fulfilled; moreover, the subject trace is associated to a referential Theta role; as such, it can be indexed under (28), hence connected over a long distance to its operator via binding. The status of (33a) is then accounted for, and it is not necessary to assume that a postverbal subject position is theta-governed.[8]

The system also accounts for the nonextractability of an NP specifier across a *wh* Comp (or another A' Specifier; see section 1.4):

(34) a ?Combien de problèmes ne sais-tu pas comment résoudre t?
       'How many problems don't you know how to solve?'
     b *Combien ne sais-tu pas comment résoudre [t de problèmes] ?
       'How many don't you know how to solve of problems?'

In (34a), the *wh* trace is in object position, a position receiving a referential Theta role; hence, an index is licit under principle (28), and long-distance construal is possible. In (34b), the trace of the extracted element is an NP specifier, a position not receiving a Theta role at all; hence, (co-)indexation is illegitimate, and the proper connection can be established only via government, an option excluded in (34b) under Relativized Minimality.

One may wonder at this point why the crucial distinction introduced by principle (28) should be stated through the mediation of Theta Theory. An alternative that comes to mind is to state it directly in terms of some naive theory of reference, or, more plausibly, in terms of the organization of what Chomsky (1981) calls "Domain D"—the universe of discourse, the cognitive domain that contains representations of what we talk about. It could be that reasons, manners, and quantities are not represented as individuals in this domain. If indices are restricted to designate individuals, the effect of (28) would be achieved, perhaps in a more straightforward way.

Still, it seems to be the case that a distinction in terms of general ontology is too crude. Some linguistic mediation is necessary. The nature of the entities involved is not the only relevant factor; the particular linguistic conceptualization of the event also seems to matter. Consider the following two sentences:

(35) a Non so se potremo dire che Gianni è stato licenziato per
       questa ragione
       'I don't know if we could say that Gianni was fired for this
       reason'
     b Non so se potremo dare questa ragione per il licenziamento
       di Gianni
       'I don't know if we could give this reason for Gianni's firing'

These two sentences are semantically quite close, in that in both cases a reason is associated to a certain event. The difference is that the reason is expressed as a lexically selected complement in (35b) and as an adjunct in (35a). Extraction from a *wh* island gives notably different results in the two cases:

(36) a *Per che ragione non sai se possiamo dire che Gianni è stato
          licenziato?
          'For what reason don't you know if we can say that Gianni
          was fired?'
       b ?Che ragione non sai se possiamo dare per il licenziamento di
          Gianni?
          'What reason don't you know if we can give for Gianni's
          firing?'

Since the entities involved are reasons in both cases, the distinction
does not seem to be directly expressible in ontological terms. What
seems to count is the specific linguistic structure chosen to express
the relation between a reason and an event. This is done by making
the reason a verbal argument in (36b) but not in (36a). In our terms,
indexation and binding are available in (36b) but not in (36a), which is
then ruled out in the relevant interpretation. It thus seems to be
necessary to mediate the licensing of indices through the particular
linguistic conceptualization of events which is expressed by Theta
Theory.

We have seen that selected PP's can be extracted from *wh* islands
on a par with NP's; on the other hand, manner and reason adverbial
PPs cannot be extracted, on a par with proper adverbial phrases. The
split cannot be made on a categorial basis; again, Theta Theory seems
to provide the right tool. Concerning the Theta marking of selected
PP's, the main property to be accounted for is the fact that the prepositional object receives a Theta role which, in a sense, is assigned
both by the verb and by the preposition; for example, we must express
the fact that a verb like *give* has a theta grid including the role *goal*,
and also the fact that this role is directly assigned by the preposition
to to the appropriate NP in VP's like *give a book to John* (Marantz
1984; Pollock 1988). We will adopt the following technique to ensure
the appropriate matching between verbal and prepositional roles: the
verb assigns a theta role to a selected PP, and this theta role must
match the one assigned by the head of the PP to its object (among
other things, through this technique the appropriate choice of the
preposition is ensured). In this way, a referential index can be licensed
on a selected PP under principle (28), thus allowing long-distance
extraction.

It has often been noted in the recent literature that different kinds
of adverb-like PP's are extractable to different degrees. In general,

nonselected locative and instrumental PP's are extractable essentially at the same level as selected PP's. Temporal PP's are more variable; they often look somewhat worse than the preceding cases, but somewhat better than manner or reason PP's. This hierarchy, which appears to be quite consistent across languages, is illustrated by the following Italian examples:

(37) a   ?In che negozio non ti ricordi che cosa abbiamo comprato?
          'In what shop don't you remember what we bought?'
     b   ?Con che chiave non ti ricordi che porta abbiamo aperto?
          'With what key don't you remember which door we
          opened?'
     c   ??A che ora non ti ricordi che cosa abbiamo detto?
          'At what time don't you remember what we said?'
     d   *In che modo non ti ricordi che cosa abbiamo detto?
          'In what way don't you remember what we said?'
     e   *Per che ragione non ti ricordi che cosa abbiamo detto?
          'For what reason don't you remember what we said?'

Instrumentals behave as selected arguments in applicative constructions in many languages (Baker 1988), so it seems appropriate to assign them the status of optionally selected arguments. If the main dividing line is to be drawn between locative and temporal phrases on the one hand and reason and manner phrases on the other, as events take place in time and space it is reasonable to assume that locative and temporal elements are selected by the head containing the event specification in the clausal structure (Higginbotham 1985). It is then conceivable that the event specification will license a temporal and locative index under (28), thus allowing long-distance construal of these elements.[9,10]

3.6   Refinements

One crucial refinement is immediately suggested by the acceptability of long-distance extraction of an adjunct from a declarative:

(38) How do you think [t' that [we can solve the problem t]] ?

This shows that a nonindexed trace does not have to be directly governed by the operator: a sequence of government relations (here between t' and t and between *how* and t') suffices to establish the connection. The theory already possesses a formal object consisting of a sequence of antecedent-government relations, the chain. Following Chomsky 1986b, I will assume that a chain is partially defined as follows:

(39) $(a_1, \ldots, a_n)$ is a chain only if, for $1 \le i < n$, a_i antecedent-governs a_{i+1}.

We now need a definition of antecedent government that does not make crucial reference to coindexation, so that it will be equally applicable to indexed and nonindexed material. We can tentatively replace the coindexation requirement of the usual definition (see section 1.3 and appendix 2 of chapter 1) with a global nondistinctness requirement (nondistinctness of indices if the elements are indexed, of category, feature content, etc.) in order to rule out the possibility of forming crazy chains (e.g., of an adjunct trace with a verb or a direct object)[11]:

(40) X antecedent-governs Y iff
   (i) X and Y are nondistinct
   (ii) X c-commands Y
   (iii) no barrier intervenes
   (iv) Relativized Minimality is respected.

On the basis of this refinement, our proposal now looks as follows. There are two (nonexclusive) ways to connect an operator and its variable: binding and a chain of government relations. Binding requires identity of referential indices, a formal property now restricted by principle (28). When coindexation and binding are not available, the chain of government relations is the only connecting device. But government relations are intrinsically local. Hence, if a link of the government chain fails, the connection between operator and variable cannot be established, and the structure is ruled out. The chain as such can cover an unbounded distance, but each link is local; this is the fundamental difference between the two connecting devices.

As the reader can easily check, the system now deals with all the fundamental asymmetries discussed in this chapter, with one important exception: the NP and clitic dependencies discussed in section 3.4. The relevant cases are the following:

(41) a   It seems that someone told Bill that . . .
     b   It seems that Bill was told t that . . .
     c   *Bill seems that it was told t that . . .

(42) a   Jean essaie [de le faire t]
         'Jean tries to do it'
     b *Jean l'essaie [de faire t]
         'Jean tries to do it'

In (41c) and (42b), the object trace receives a referential theta role, an index is licit, hence the connection with the antecedent can be established over a long distance via binding, and the ill-formedness of these examples does not seem to be amenable to a unitary treatment with the familiar asymmetries in our system. In fact, this case looks different irrespective of the particular analysis that one adopts for the extractions from *wh* islands. It just seems to be the case that in A-type antecedent-trace dependencies (which include clitic dependencies, we assume) the argument-adjunct distinction, which pervasively characterizes A' dependencies, is wiped out, and all A dependencies obey the strong locality conditions which are restricted to adjuncts in A' dependencies. Why should it be so? The natural thing to do is to try to relate this strong asymmetry to some independent difference between the two types of dependencies. The most conspicuous difference concerns Theta Theory: antecedent-trace dependencies of the A type typically relate an argument to a thematic position; hence, some sort of transmission of theta role must be involved.

A frequently adopted, straightforward way to properly state this kind of theta-role inheritance without implying an actual transmission is to formulate the Theta Criterion directly in terms of the notion chain, along the following lines:

(43) **Theta Criterion**
     (i) Each Theta position belongs to a chain containing exactly
         one argument.
     (ii) Each argument belongs to a chain containing exactly one
         Theta position.

Following a suggestion due to Norbert Hornstein (see also note 24 of Aoun et al. 1987), and developing in a different way an intuition also underlying Williams' (1987) approach, we can then claim that (41c) and (42b) are ill formed not for a generic failure to connect antecedent and trace but for the failure of the specific connection required by Theta Theory: if the Theta Criterion is defined in terms of chain, and chain is defined in terms of antecedent government, as in (39), then in (41c) and (42b) the object theta role cannot be assigned to the appropriate formal object (a chain containing the arguments *Bill* and *le*, respectively); hence, these structures violate the Theta Criterion. No such effect arises for A' dependencies, which do not involve any sort of Theta-role inheritance and in fact are not affected by Theta Theory at all.

In short: The strong locality conditions holding in A' dependencies with adjuncts and in all A dependencies can be unified and traced back to a common source, the antecedent-government condition on chains. But chain formation is enforced for different reasons in the two cases. In the first case, it is the only connecting device available; in the second case, it is the specific connecting device required by Theta Theory. The fundamental difference between the two cases—the fact that the argument-adjunct distinction is obliterated in A dependencies—is related to an independent asymmetry between the two types of dependency: their different status with respect to Theta Theory. With A dependencies, a chain connection is required in all cases for theta-theoretic reasons.[12]

Another important refinement is argued for by Cinque (1989), who points out that the possibility of long-distance construal via binding is a function not only of the presence of a referential theta role but also of the nature of the moved element, which must possess some intrinsic referential property: it must allow discourse linking in the sense of Pesetsky 1987. Roughly speaking, a quantified expression is discourse-linked when its variable has a range fixed in the previous discourse, a property that depends in part on the form of the expression (e.g., it is favored if the quantified NP contains a lexical N'). For instance, the Italian quantified expression *qualcosa* (something), an expression strongly disfavoring discourse linking, allows long-distance A' movement but disallows extraction from a *wh* island, even when it is construed with a referential Theta role:

(44) a Qualcosa, credo che farà t
        'Something, I believe he will do t'
     b *Qualcosa, mi domando se farà t
        'Something, I wonder whether he will do t'

Cinque proposes that the principle licensing referential indices must be made sensitive to the nature of the theta position *and of its filler at D-structure*, which must possess the potential for discourse linking. Reference to the presence and the nature of the theta role must be maintained for such facts as (36), and for the general fact that manner and reason adverbials remain nonextractable also in the form *P what N'*, which as such would permit discourse linking (the improvement that some speakers find in this case—see note 10—could now be related to the fact that one of the two conditions for indexation is met; see Cinque 1989 for a detailed discussion of this improvement).

3.7   On Some "Surprising Asymmetries"

3.7.1   Intermediate Traces within Islands
Some additional remarks are demanded by paradigm (19), repeated here for convenience:

(45) a ?*Who do you wonder [whether [we believe [t' [t can help us]]]]

 b ??Who do you wonder [whether [we believe [(t') [we can help t]]]]

 c *How do you wonder [whether [we believe [(t') [we can help Bill t]]]]

In (45c), the variable t should be connected to its operator *how*. Binding being unavailable, a chain of antecedent-government relations is the only option. t' antecedent-governs t, but *how* is too far away to antecedent-govern t'. The connection thus fails, and the structure is not interpretable (whether or not t' is actually present). In (45b), indexing is licensed under (28); hence, the connection between *who* and t can be established via binding. Under the current account, the presence of t' is irrelevant: a trace in Comp is not needed to establish the required connections, and its presence does not give rise to an ECP violation *per se* (as it did under the theory of section 3.1), since it is properly head-governed by the higher verb. Thus, its presence is optional (but see below). Consider now (45a). Indexing is licit; hence, (45a) can be connected to its variable t through binding, as in the preceding case. But in this case the presence of t' is necessary to induce C^0 agreement, which allows satisfaction of the proper-head-government requirement for t under the proposal of section 2.5. Thus the ECP is satisfied, the proper operator-variable connection can be established through binding (a referential index being legitimate under (28)), and the example is treated on a par with (45b)—a desirable result in view of its level of acceptability.

It remains to be determined why Pesetsky's surprising asymmetries exist. Why is it that subject extraction in this environment is somewhat worse than object extraction? Neither our reduced ECP nor the connection requirement can be responsible for this subtle but systematic contrast. The crucial difference that we can capitalize on seems to be the obligatory presence of the trace in Comp in the case of subject extraction. Why should the presence of this trace determine a slight degradation?

As Pesetsky (1984) originally pointed out, this seems to be a particular case of a general pattern: whenever an extraction process from an island takes place, if the construction requires the postulation of an intermediate trace higher than the variable and free within the island, the structure is more deviant than a structure not requiring the intermediate trace, all other things being equal. For instance, Browning (1987) finds a parallel degradation in cases of long-distance extraction of subjects from (declaratives embedded within) *wh* islands and complex noun phrases. Thus, if the brackets designate an island in (46), it appears that, all other things being equal, (46a) is more degraded than (46b).

(46) a Op . . . [. . . t . . . vbl . . .
     b Op . . . [. . . vbl . .

Similar facts have been pointed out for parasitic gap structures (Pesetsky 1984; Stowell 1986; Browning 1987). The following examples are adapted from Browning's dissertation:

(47) a   *The professor that you consulted t because you thought
            that t understood the problem
     b   ??The professor that you consulted t because you thought t
            understood the problem
     c   ?The problem that you presented t because you thought he
            understood t

(47a) involves a violation of the head-government requirement, and appears to be significantly worse than the other cases, as expected. In (47c) no trace in the intermediate Comp of the parasitic gap structure is required; in (47b) such an intermediate trace is necessary to license agreement in Comp, which ensures proper head government of the subject trace. The degradation observed in this pair is analogous to the other cases. This case can be assimilated to the descriptive generalization expressed in (46) under the chain-composition analysis of Chomsky (1986b) as revised by Browning (1987).

In addition to long-distance extraction (or chain composition) from islands and parasitic gaps, at least two more cases are reported in the literature which appear to be amenable to the same descriptive generalization.

The first case concerns the Romance construction involving *wh* extraction of the subject of an infinitival complement, discussed in section 2.5:

(48) a   Un homme que je pense que tu crois [t Agr [t être capable de faire cela]]
         'A man that I think that you believe to be capable of doing this'

     b   ??Un homme que je ne sais pas si tu connais bien t
         'A man that I don't know if you know well'

     c   ?*Un homme que je ne sais pas si tu crois [t Agr [t être capable de faire cela]]
         'A man who I don't know if you believe to be capable of doing this'

     d   *Un homme que je ne sais pas si t pourra faire cela
         'A man who I don't know if will be able to do that'

Extraction of the subject of the infinitive across a *wh* island as in (48c) is degraded in comparison with (48b), a case of simple object extraction. Still, for many speakers it is clearly better than a case of adjunct extraction, or a case of subject extraction involving a violation of the head-government requirement, as in (48d). (A similar judgment holds in Italian if the equivalent of (48c) is compared with a case of adjunct extraction.)

The second case involves the *que qui* rule in French. Its application inside a *wh* island produces a deviant result, as in (49c):

(49) a   L'homme que je pense que tu crois [t qui [t viendra]]
         'The man that I think that you believe that will come'

     b   ??L'homme que je ne sais pas si tu connais bien t
         'The man who I don't know if you know well'

     c   ?*L'homme que je ne sais pas si tu crois [t qui [t viendra]]
         'The man that I don't know if you believe that will come'

     d   *L'homme que je ne sais pas si t viendra
         'The man who I don't know if will come'

(49c) is degraded with respect to (49a) (subject extraction from a declarative across another declarative) and (49b) (object extraction from a *wh* island), but is far better than (49d), which involves a violation of the head-government requirement.[13]

Why should this surprising degradation effect hold? I would like to tentatively propose the following, in the spirit of Chomsky's (1988) least-effort guidelines. Suppose that an element can legitimately occur at LF only if it is licensed by an interpretation or, more broadly, if it plays an active role on this level. Within the A′ system, "playing an active role at LF" means being either an operator, an operator-bound variable, or an intermediate trace that participates in establishing a chain connection between an operator and a variable. Thus, an intermediate trace in Comp is allowed to occur at LF in examples like those in (50) because it plays an active role: it participates in the A′-chain connecting the operator and its variable.[14]

(50) a Who do you think [t [t came]] ?
      b Who do you think [t [he saw t]] ?
      c How do you think [t [he spoke t]] ?

In this respect, the situation is different in cases like (45a): there the trace in Comp must be left behind when movement applies in order to allow the presence of C^0 Agr, necessary for the familiar reasons. But it is neither a variable, nor an operator, nor an intermediate link of a chain connecting a variable and an operator; it cannot be governed by its antecedent, which is too far away, and therefore no chain connection can be established. As the elements involved have a referential theta role, a binding connection can be established; hence the structure is not as bad as a case of adjunct extraction. But the presence of the intermediate trace at LF is illegitimate under our interpretation of Chomsky's least-effort guidelines for the A′ system. The same conclusion holds for t′ in (45b), but in this case there is the option of not leaving the trace when movement applies, which overcomes the problem. Thus, the "surprising asymmetry," which in our terms cannot be due to the ECP or to a failure to establish the required connection, can be attributed to the fact that (45a) fails to meet a natural optimality condition on LF. It is possible to intepret the facts of (47), (48), (49), and the other cases instantiating the abstract structure (46)a in a similar vein.[15]

3.7.2 An Interpretive Asymmetry

My proposal departs from Chomsky's approach in one respect: it assumes that intermediate traces of arguments can be represented at LF, provided that a chain of antecedent government relations holds. So, in (51a) the operator can be connected to its variable in two ways (through government and through binding), whereas in (51b) the connection can be established in only one way (through binding), as government fails under relativized minimality.

(51) a   What book do you think [t that [John gave t to Bill]]
     b   ?What book do you wonder [why [John gave t to Bill]]

If this difference is represented at LF, we may expect, in principle, that interpretive differences can materialize between the two cases. One important difference in fact exists: Longobardi (1984) has shown that certain phenomena of scope reconstruction exist when the operator-variable connection is established through chain, but not when it can be established only via binding, in our terms. This contrast can be illustrated by the interpretive properties of structures like the following:

(52) Tell me what everyone gave t to Bill on his birthday

This sentence manifests a well-known scope ambiguity, with either *What* or *everyone* taking wide scope ("Tell me what is the thing such that everyone gave it to Bill" and "Tell me, for each individual involved, what is the thing that he gave to Bill"); see May 1985 for discussion. The ambiguity still holds if the *wh* element is moved to a higher clause (Williams 1986); (53) can have the interpretation in which different people should choose different gifts.

(53) Tell me what you think that everyone should give to Bill

As an operator in an embedded subject position cannot directly take scope over a superordinate Comp (i.e., *Tell me who thinks that everyone left* cannot mean "Tell me for every individual who thinks that he left"), we must conclude that in (53) scope reconstruction is operative—i.e., that *what* behaves, for scope interaction, as if it was in the embedded clause. (See Aoun and Li 1989 for a technique of scope assignment that deals directly with these cases.) Now, this sort of scope reconstruction is restricted to cases in which the operator is chain-connected to its variable; if the government chain cannot be construed, and only the binding relation can be established, reconstruction is excluded. Compare (53) with the following:

(54) a   Tell me what you don't think that everyone should give to Bill
     b   Tell me what you regret that everyone gave to Bill
     c   ?Tell me what you wonder why everyone gave to Bill

    d ??Tell me what you heard rumors that everyone wanted to
      give to Bill

A chain connection is excluded in (54a) by the intervening negation, in (54b) by the fact that the spec of Comp with factive verbs is not available for an intermediate trace, in (54c) by the intervening *wh* Comp, and in (54d) by the barrier associated to the complex NP structure. In none of these cases is scope reconstruction permissible; that is, none of them seems to be compatible with an interpretation in which different people gave or should give different presents to Bill. Thus, it appears that scope reconstruction is restricted to government chains, and never appears in cases in which long-distance binding is the only available construal. Cinque (1989) argues that this is simply due to the fact that the long-distance binding connection requires an intrinsic referential quality of the moved element, a necessary condition to license the appropriate referential index (see the end of section 3.6); this intrinsic referential quality is incompatible with a genuine quantificational interpretation, necessary for a narrow-scope interpretation.[16]

On the basis of these interpretive asymmetries, we are led to conclude that A' connections involving argument variables can in principle be established at LF both via government chains and via binding; therefore, intermediate traces chain-connecting argument variables to their operators must be allowed to appear in LF. We thus have evidence to extend Chomsky's full interpretation guideline to allow the LF occurrence of three kinds of elements within the A' system: operators, variables, and intermediate traces participating in government connections (the latter legitimately occurring irrespective of the argumental or nonargumental nature of the variable); we can then maintain that the degraded status of (45a) and of all the other cases instantiating (46a) is due to the obligatory presence of an intermediate trace which cannot be integrated into an A'-chain and which hence does not meet (our interpretation of) Chomsky's guidelines.

3.7.3 ECM Subjects

A final potentially relevant fact is the status of extraction of exceptional case-marking subjects from *wh* islands:

(55) This is a man who I wonder [whether you believe [t to be
     intelligent]]

There is some disagreement in the literature on this issue. Koopman and Sportiche (1988) consider them on a par with object extractions and, on the basis of this judgment, motivate a modification of their approach. Similarly, Chomsky (1982, 1986b) and Lasnik and Saito (1984) implicitly classify this case with object extraction, and explicitly contrast it with subject extraction from a tensed clause in parasitic gap structures (their diacritics):

(56) a   Someone who John expected t to be successful though believing [t to be incompetent]

    b   ?*Someone who John expected t would be successful though believing [t [t is incompetent]]

This contrast is expected under our approach to the surprising asymmetries: in (56a) no intermediate trace must (or can) appear within the parasitic gap structure; hence, the factor determining the degraded status of (56b) is absent.

On the other hand, Pesetsky (1984), Stowell (1986), and Browning (1987) discuss a number of cases involving extraction from an island (or in a parasitic gap structure) of a subject of an ECM clause, which they find degraded with respect to object extraction. For instance, Browning mentions the following subtle contrast (her diacritics):

(57) a   ??The horse that you bet on t because you expected to win the race

    b   ?The horse that you bet on t because you expected Bill to ride

Our approach to the "surprising asymmetries" is silent on this kind of asymmetry, as examples like (57a) do not involve any intermediate trace within the island or parasitic gap structure. Two questions are raised by this new subtle asymmetry: Where does it come from? Should it receive a fully unified analysis with (45), etc.? It seems to me that the answer to the second question should be negative, as for many speakers there is a weak but systematic contrast between extraction of the subject of a tensed declarative and extraction of an ECM infinitive in the relevant contexts:

(58) a   ??This is the person who I forgot whether John believes [t to have proved the theorem]

    b   ?*This is the person who I forgot whether John believes [t [t has proved the theorem]]

What, then, could be the additional factor detected by Pesetsky, Stowell, and Browning? One possibility is to further integrate the core of the approach to long extraction defended by Koopman and Sportiche (1988), who argue for the following empirical generalization: long extraction (i.e., in their terms, extraction from a clause without passing through its Comp) is possible only from a Theta position. We could incorporate their insight (and nuance it in accordance with the weakness of the observed effect) in the following manner: a long-distance binding connection gives optimally acceptable results when the variable is in the referential thematic position which licenses the referential index, and is marked otherwise; if we assume (see Koopman and Sportiche 1988 and references cited there) that the spec of IP (the only possible site for subject extraction in languages like English) is always a derived, nonthematic position, it follows that long-distance subject extraction across an island will always be more marked than object extraction, whether the extracted element is the subject of a tensed clause or of an ECM infinitive.

According to this refinement, the theory of referential indices allows an optimal application of the binding strategy with long-distance extraction of nonsubject arguments, in which case the variable occupies the position in which the index is licensed, and a marked application with extraction of subjects (in languages like English and French, in which a subject is never extracted from a Theta position, according to Koopman and Sportiche (1988)), due to the mismatch between the position in which the index is licensed and the position of the variable; the binding strategy continues to be inapplicable with adjunct extraction, as no index is licensed in this case (this gradation further interacts with the dimension introduced by Cinque's proposal, having to do with the inherent referential quality of the extracted element).

In conclusion: At least four distinct levels of acceptability—depending on the nature of the extraction site—appear to be detectable in cases of A′ subject extraction from a clause in English, ranging from fully acceptable to severely ill formed:

A. extraction of the subject of a declarative across a null complementizer;

B. extraction of the subject of an ECM clause embedded within a *wh* island, violating Bounding Theory and making a marked use of the binding strategy (the variable is not in the Theta position licensing the referential index);

C. extraction of the subject of a tensed declarative (or of the infinitival Romance construction) embedded within a *wh* island, violating Bounding Theory, making a marked use of the binding strategy, and requiring an illicit intermediate trace;

D. extraction of the subject of the *wh* island, which, in addition to other violations, violates the head-government requirement, determining a much stronger deviance than the other factors.

Extraction of an object from a *wh* island has a status somehow intermediate between A and B, as it only involves a violation of Bounding Theory. Extraction of an adjunct from a *wh* island gives a result about as bad as D (to the extent that the two kinds of violations are comparable); in that case neither the government nor the binding connection can be established between operator and variable, and the result is total unacceptability. Although the status of the extreme points of the hierarchy is stable across speakers and lexically invariable, the subtle distinctions between the intermediate degrees appear sensitive to individual variation and affected by the lexical choices, as is pointed out in the references mentioned in connection with these cases. The hierarchy is, in essence, preserved with other islands (or parasitic gap constructions), with the absolute values affected by the specific strength of the island, and with the relational values held fundamentally constant.

3.8   Conclusions

Referential indices were introduced in syntactic theory to encode referential dependencies between arguments. In the spirit of the original proposal, I have argued that their use should be restricted to elements associated to referential theta roles. This move has the effect of significantly limiting the availability of binding as a bookkeeping device to express relations of various sorts. In the domain of A' relations, binding can now only express the dependencies involving referential variables, in the sense made precise through Theta Theory. Variables which are nonreferential in this sense (adverbs lexically selected or not, measure phrases, idiom chunks, . . .) cannot be connected to their operators via binding, and must exploit the other connecting device offered by the system: government. Therefore, this second kind of A′ dependency can be expressed only via a chain of government relations. Binding can take place at an unbounded distance, provided that its two components (identity of referential indices and c-command) are met. Government, on the other hand, is intrinsically local. I have argued that this fundamental difference is the source of the familiar argument-adjunct asymmetries with respect to island sensitivity. An adjunct variable can never be connected to its operator via binding, because of its nonreferential nature; and it cannot be connected via government across an island, because one of the necessary government relations inevitably fails, owing to Relativized Minimality and/or the presence of a barrier. No connection can be established, and such structures are ruled out as uninterpretable. On the contrary, a referential variable can always be connected to its operator via binding, a relation not affected by island barriers and Minimality. The island sensitivity thus gives rise to less dramatic effects in this case, and is manifested only by the marginality arising from a violation of Subjacency or other relatively weak principles and conditions.

Appendix 1   Adverbial PP Preposing

The possibility of extracting an adverbial element from a *wh* island seems to depend in part on the nature of the construction. Simple preposing of an adverbial PP gives an almost fully acceptable result in Italian; compare (59) with the ill-formed case of *wh* extraction (60):

(59) a   Per questa ragione, non immagino chi potrebbe essere licenziato
'For this reason, I don't imagine who could be fired'
   b   In questo modo, non immagino chi potrebbe essersi comportato
'In this way, I don't imagine who could have behaved'

(60) a   *Per quale ragione non immagini chi potrebbe essere licenziato?
'For what reason do you not imagine who could be fired?'
   b   *In che modo non immagini chi potrebbe essersi comportato?
'In what way don't you imagine who could have behaved?'

(Nonrestrictive relatives tend to pattern with simple preposing; clefts, focal topicalization, and restrictive relatives are somewhere in between. Richard Kayne independently noticed somewhat similar effects in English.) Two possible tacks can be explored to deal with such contrasts.

One could take advantage of the intuitively more referential character of the preposed phrase in (59), and make the referential index (almost) fully legitimate in such cases through a revision of the licensing principle, possibly along the lines of a combination of note 10 and Cinque's (1989) proposal.

Alternatively, one could maintain the assumption that a referential index is not licit in such cases, owing to the lack of a referential theta role; a chain of government relations would still be required to establish the proper connection in (59). One could then capture the distinction between (59) and (60) through a further refinement of Relativized Minimality: informally, an A' specifier filled by an operator blocks an antecedent-government relation in an A'-chain only if the latter itself involves an operator-variable configuration, as in (60); as the preposing in (59) presumably does not involve an operator-variable configuration (Cinque, forthcoming), the intervening A' specifier does not block an antecedent-government relation. (The PP can be moved in one fell swoop or through successive adjunctions, depending on other considerations; Obenauer (forthcoming) discusses a blocking principle having such a selective effect.)

Evidence for the second alternative seems to be provided by the fact that adverbial PP's are not extractable by simple preposing from other weak islands, such as the complements of factive verbs, which in general allow extraction of an argumental PP:

(61) a *Per questa ragione, rimpiango che sia stato licenziato
        'For this reason, I regret that he was fired'
     b *In questo modo, mi dispiace che si sia comportato con tutti
        'In this way, I regret that he behaved with everyone'

(The asterisk on (61a) refers, of course, to the long-distance construal of the PP.) If this kind of simple preposing of adverbial needs a chain of antecedent-government relations, the examples of (61) are excluded by the fact that an intrinsic barrier, the boundary of the factive complement, fatally blocks a crucial antecedent-government relation. If, on the other hand, one were to assume that a referential index is licit in these cases, and that hence a long-distance binding relation can be established in (59), etc., the impossibility of (61) would remain mysterious. We thus have an argument for dealing with (59) through a refinement of Relativized Minimality, rather than a refinement of the licensing of referential indices.[17]

The asymmetry between (59) and (61) argues against a close assimilation of the two types of weak islands (e.g. through the assumption that factive complements involve some kind of factive operator filling the Spec of C position), and seems to support the view that factive complements are intrinsic barriers.

Appendix 2   Extraction from NP (and PP)

Although in English things are somewhat blurred by the option of stranding a preposition, the fundamental empirical generalization governing extraction from NP in Romance languages is quite clear: only the subject of the NP, a nominal which can occupy the possessive position, can be extracted. This generalization, originally arrived at by Cinque (1980) for Italian (see Milner (1982) on French), has given rise to an important theoretical debate (Aoun 1985; Chomsky 1986b; Torrego 1985; Giorgi and Longobardi 1987; Pollock 1988). A full discussion of the issue goes well beyond our present purposes. This appendix is simply meant to illustrate what direction of analysis our current framework of assumptions would lead us to take. First, I will briefly illustrate the empirical core of the issue.

Only genitive nominal complements (= *di NP*) can be extracted from NP's:

(62) a   Il missile di cui ho fotografato [l'atterraggio t]
         'The missile of which I photographed the landing'
     b   L'uomo politico di cui ho registrato [la telefonata t]
         'The politician by whom I recorded the phone call'
     c   Gianni, del quale ho ammirato [il regalo t]
         'Gianni, of whom I admired the present'

(63) a   *Il pianeta su cui ho fotografato [l'atterraggio t]
         'The planet on which I photographed the landing'
     b   *L'uomo politico a cui ho registrato [la telefonata t]
         'The politician to whom I recorded the phone call'
     c   *Gianni, per il quale ho ammirato [il regalo t]
         'Gianni, for whom I admired the present'

As only genitive NP's, when pronominal, can become possessives, it is natural to think that extraction from NP is possible only through the possessive position. This is confirmed by Cinque's observation that when the possessive position is filled, even an otherwise extractable genitive NP cannot be extracted. (See the references cited for detailed discussion.) Why is it, then, that extraction from NP must necessarily pass through the NP specifier,[18] as in (64)?

(64) XP . . . . [t [N^0 . . . t . . .]]

As the extracted elements are referential in the relevant sense, the connection between the antecedent and the trace can always be established via binding. Hence, within our frame of assumptions there is no way to enforce a sequence of antecedent-government relations on such grounds. (Thanks to Anna Szabolcsi for raising this problem in connection with her analysis of the Hungarian NP; see Szabolcsi 1987.) The natural alternative is the head-government requirement: we could explore the possibility that the severe constraints on extraction from NP are a consequence of the failure of proper head government on the extraction site in many cases. (See Longobardi 1987 for a detailed proposal along similar lines.)

The structure of the argument will be as follows. Nouns are defective governors in various respects, and as such are unable to fulfill the head-government requirement on a trace when one of their complements is moved. But if the moved complement passes through the Specifier of N, something happens which turns the noun into a sufficient governor. Phrased in such a way, this case bears a close resemblance to the case of extraction of the subject of a clause: in both cases, the fact that the extracted element passes through the immediately higher specifier has the effect of turning the specifier's head into an appropriate governor. The analogy immediately suggests a candidate for this change of status: spec-head agreement. This process seems to have the capacity to convert an intrinsically inadequate head into an element appropriate for fulfilling the head-government requirement on traces.

Let us review the reasons why nouns should be inadequate governors in the relevant sense. First, cross-clausal NP movement in passive and raising cannot take place within NP's (Kayne 1984, chapter 3):

(65) a *John's appearance [t to be sick]
      b *John's belief [t (to be) sick]

Second, P stranding under NP movement is impossible in NP's:

(66) *The new law's vote [for t]

(consider *The new law was voted for* and *The vote for the new law*). Third, verbs license a null complementizer in their tensed complements, whereas nouns do not (Kayne 1984, chapter 3; Stowell 1981):

(67) a I believe (that) she is a genius
     b The belief *(that) she is genius

Kayne (1984) claimed that nouns are nonstructural governors, i.e., that their governing capacity does not extend beyond their subcategorization frame. This could be looked at as an inherent property of nouns, or as a consequence of the proper definition of barrier for government. Taking the second option, I will adopt Cinque's (forthcoming) proposal to the effect that a maximal projection not selected by a $[+V]$ head is a barrier:

(68) XP is a barrier if it is not directly selected by an X^0 nondistinct from $[+V]$.

(68) implies that nouns, contrary to verbs and adjectives (on prepositions see below) will never be able to govern inside a lower maximal projection. Then the observed facts follow: in (65) the (small) clausal boundaries will block government from the noun, and these structures will systematically violate the head-government requirement on the subject traces; in (66) no problem arises for head government, as prepositions are adequate head governors in English; but we know that A-dependencies require antecedent government for proper thematic transmission (see section 3.6); hence, the intervening PP barrier will block the required antecedent-government relation. As for (67), if a null (tensed) C^0 requires head government (Stowell 1981; Kayne 1984), the presence of the CP barrier will rule out the structure.

A possible way to interpret the facts of (62)-(63) and the relevant empirical generalization would be to claim that elements distinct from $[+V]$ not only are unable to free a complement from barrierhood but also are insufficient head governors for traces. This would, in essence, keep the intuition behind various versions of the connectedness approach (Kayne 1984 and much subsequent work) and Huang's (1982) CED, according to which the structural conditions on a trace and on the extraction domains are fundamentally homogeneous—an intuition developed in great detail in the system of Cinque (forthcoming). Suppose, then, that our proper-head-government requirement is strengthened to the effect that a $[-V]$ element must be reinforced by (abstract) agreement in order to fulfill the head-government requirement on a trace. This gives the effect illustrated in (64): the extracted element must pass through the Spec of the NP in order to trigger abstract agreement on the head, which turns the nominal element into an appropriate head governor for the trace. It then follows that nongenitive elements, which cannot pass through the Spec position because of their Case properties, or genitive elements in structures in which the spec position is already filled, cannot be extracted from NP, as their traces could not be properly head-governed.

This approach must assume that agreement makes a $[-V]$ element a proper governor for a trace, but it does not suffice to allow the $[-V]$ element to free its complement from barrierhood; otherwise the ill-formed structures of (65) and (66) would be ruled in. A careful look at the relevant structures shows that this does not really imply a primitive asymmetry between the conditions on the tace and the conditions on extraction domains: under the natural assumption that an agreement specification governs only elements coindexed with it, agreement on the noun, coindexed with its spec and the spec's trace, does not govern the clausal or PP complement. The latter is governed only by the noun, a $[-V]$ governor inadequate to free it from barrierhood. Hence, a barrier intervenes between the agreeing noun and the trace, and the proper-head-government requirement is violated.[19]

If traces must be properly head governed by $[+V]$, as Cinque (forthcoming) points out, we have an immediate account of the fact that most languages do not allow preposition-stranding. Consider this example from Italian:

(69) *Chi hai parlato [a t] ?
    'Who did you talk to?'

The preposition, specified $[-V, -N]$, does not properly head-govern the trace; moreover, it blocks (proper) government from the verb, under Minimality. For the analysis of stranding languages, such as English, I would like to follow the spirit of Pollock's (1988) proposal according to which the stranding option is related to the fact that English prepositions are underspecified with respect to the features $[\pm V, \pm N]$. But, rather than assuming that English prepositions are (can be) nondistinct from nouns (as in Pollock's system), I would like to execute this idea in a way much closer to Kayne's (1984) original approach to the Stranding parameter, and assume that English prepositions "govern and assign Case like verbs" because they are not distinct from verbs (i.e., $[-N]$ and not specified with respect to the feature $[\pm V]$). As such, they count as proper governors and license a trace.[20]

As nouns can become appropriate governors for traces when they are reinforced by agreement, one may wonder whether the same procedure could be used to allow extraction from (fully specified) prepositions in some languages. Such languages should have the Spec of PP available for movement of the prepositional object, which would trigger (abstract) head agreement while passing through Spec and allow P^0 to properly govern its trace:

(70) XP . . . . [t [P^0 t]]

This appears to be the pattern of preposition-stranding in Dutch, according to the description and analysis of Van Riemsdijk (1978): a prepositional object can be moved to the Spec of P, where it receives locative case; then it can be extracted from this position. It follows that only elements that allow locative case marking can be *wh*-extracted from PP's, just as only elements allowing genitive case marking can be extracted from NP in Romance languages. In both cases extraction can take place only through the Spec position, because only in this way is it possible to fulfill the head-government requirement within a $[-V]$ projection. In both cases, the only extractable elements are those compatible with the specific case-marking properties of the Spec position.

Notes

Chapter 1

1. In Chomsky's system, g is a barrier for b in (i)

(i) . . . a . . . [$_g$ . . . d . . . b . . .] . . .

if g is (a projection, the immediate projection) of d, a zero-level category distinct from b. See pp. 42ff. of Chomsky 1986b for a discussion of the consequences of this view of Minimality, and for the empirical differences between a definition assuming g to be the *immediate* projection of d and one assuming it to be *any* projection of d.

2. Various other approaches have been suggested in the recent literature to deal with the adjunct-argument asymmetries; see Cinque 1984, Obenauer 1984, Lasnik and Saito 1984, Chomsky 1986b, Longobardi (forthcoming), and Rizzi 1988. Here we have initially selected the Theta-government approach for concreteness. See chapter 3 for a detailed discussion of the issue.

3. X m-commands Y (or c-commands Y à la Aoun and Sportiche 1981) iff neither X dominates Y nor vice versa, and the first maximal projection dominating X dominates Y as well. X c-commands Y iff neither X dominates Y nor vice versa, and the first projection dominating X dominates Y as well (I differ here from Reinhart (1976) and agree with Sportiche (1988b) in not requiring that the relevant projection branch). The fact that head government requires m-command and antecedent government requires c-command appears to be an irreducible difference between government and binding (e.g., in NP's we want the head noun to govern its specifier for Case assignment, but a complement is unable to bind the specifier (see Giorgi 1985): government *per se* involves m-command, binding *per se* involves c-command; hence, antecedent government, which simultaneously involves government and binding, must refer to the more restrictive notion of c-command.

4. For instance, we need a hierarchical definition to block government of a prepositional object from a verb in a verb-final language:

(i) . . . [$_{VP}$ [$_{PP}$ P NP] V]

as well as in many other cases in which a linear definition would fail. If intervention is hierarchically defined in terms of c-command, we obtain the result hat, as a specifier is not c-commanded by its head, it will never be protected from external government. On the other hand, if we had defined intervention in terms of m-command, a specifier would always be protected from external government, as its head would always intervene between the specifier and an external governor. Perhaps a mixed definition is in order. As far as the specifiers of nonlexical heads are concerned, we clearly need the definition in the text: the Spec of I, the subject, must be accessible to government from C, the Spec of C must be accessible to government from a higher V, and so on. On the other hand, in some cases the specifiers of lexical heads appear to be protected from external government; see subsection 2.3.2 and section 3.4. We will tentatively assume that this is the case in general; hence, intervention must be defined in terms of c-command for functional heads and in terms of m-command for lexical heads. This essentially amounts to building Longobardi's (1987) uniqueness constraint on government into Relativized Minimality. See also the end of section 2.6 below, appendix 2 of chapter 3 below, and Giorgi and Longobardi 1987.

5. Rigid minimality triggered by N^0 blocks adjunct extraction from complex NP's in the system of Chomsky 1986b (p. 43):

(i) *How did John announce [a plan [t' [PRO to fix the car t]]]

Relativized Minimality does not deal with this case. Cinque (forthcoming) points out that if sentential complements of nouns generally are intrinsic barriers (see note 6 below), the antecedent-government requirement on t' will inevitably fail for reasons independent from minimality.

6. Adjunct extraction gives rise to robust violations when it takes place from islands not involving A' specifiers—sentential subjects, sentential complements of nouns, adverbial clauses, and even very weak islands such as the complements of factive verbs:

 (i) *How do you believe that to solve the problem t should be possible

 (ii) *How do you believe the claim that he solved the problem t

(iii) *How did you go to MIT to solve the problem t

(iv) *How do you regret that he solved the problem t

Here Relativized Minimality does not seem to be relevant, because there is no obvious intervening potential A' governor for the adjunct trace. This suggests that minimality is not the only constraint on government, and there is an independent notion of barrier blocking government relations, as in Chomsky 1986b. In fact, this notion is kept in our definitions of head government and antecedent government. For our purposes, it is sufficient to assume the following minimal definition of barrier for government, adapted from Cinque (forthcoming):

(v) XP is a barrier if it is not directly selected by an X^0 not distinct from [+V].

(Here "select" means "s-select" (Theta mark) for lexical heads and c-select for functional heads; subjects are not directly selected by V^0, but by VP; for the case of factive verbs, we assume the analysis of Kiparsky and Kiparsky (1971) according to which the sentential complement is immediately dominated by an NP node, which protects it from direct selection from the verb; see Acquaviva 1989 for an improved approach.) Various refinements are needed, e.g. to make the boundaries of the subject of a small clause transparent for government (Chomsky 1986b, p. 85). See Cinque (forthcoming) for an insightful discussion of these cases, and of the possibility of formulating a partially unified theory of government and bounding based on such a simplified notion of barrier and Relativized Minimality. Following Cinque's discussion, we could assume that C^0 and I^0 are not distinct from $[+V]$, and hence the XP's they select, IP and VP, never are intrinsic barriers; alternatively, it could be the case that IP and VP are intrinsic barriers, and their barrierhood can be selectively voided through the techniques discussed in Chomsky 1986b (with adjunction now applicable to IP). This alternative is left open here.

7. Browning (1989) points out that if an extended chain of agreement relations involving intervening heads is established in structures with derived subjects, as in (ia) below, it is not obvious how (ib) and other violations of the Head Movement Constraint could be explained by the ECP, as the trace of *have* would be antecedent governed by *must* in the extended chain.

(i) a   They$_i$ must$_i$ have$_i$ been$_i$ arrested$_i$ t$_i$
    b   *Have they must t been arrested t

8. The fundamental cases requiring the inheritance clause of the definition of Barrier in Chomsky (1986b)—(18) and (26)—can thus be subsumed under Relativized Minimality, which makes the inheritance clause apparently dispensable for the theory of government.

Rigid Minimality can achieve the same effect as Relativized Minimality on (26) if it is assumed that an intervening empty C^0 suffices to trigger the principle. But this would have consequences for the analysis of the *that*-trace effect under Rigid Minimality. See section 2.2.

9. Obenauer gives several arguments showing that structures like (27b) are genuine violations of the Left Branch Constraint and cannot be derived through PP extraposition from structures like (27a). That is, the following representation is impossible:

(i) *[Combien t] a-t-il consulté t [de livres]

This claim is supported by Kayne's (1985) analysis of past participle agreement: only when the whole direct object is moved do we find past-participle agreement, as is particularly clear with verbs in which agreement is audible:

(ii) Combien de voitures a-t-il conduit*es*
     'How many of cars has he driven(plur)'

(iii) Combien a-t-il conduit de voitures
     'How many has he driven(sing) of cars'

If the only possible representation of (iii) is the one corresponding to (27b), then these facts follow from Kayne's analysis: the QP *combien* cannot be moved, because of structure preservation, through the VP-external NP position which triggers agreement. This simple explanation would not be available if a representation like (i) was possible for (iii): the NP [*combien* t] should be allowed to pass through the VP-external position and trigger agreement. In turn, the impossibility of representation (i) can be attributed to the ECP, as the trace of *de livres* would not meet the head-government requirement (on which see subsection 2.3.3).

10. Obenauer shows that (28) and (29b) are closely related, and that the latter is, in a sense, parasitic on the former. See also chapter 3 of Kayne 1984; Milner 1978.

11. Following Emonds 1976 and Pollock 1989, I will assume that the inflected verb or auxiliary is moved to Infl in tensed clauses. This gives the order Aux—Spec of VP—V illustrated in (28). The hypothesis that *beaucoup* is the A′ specifier of the VP is incompatible with the idea that the thematic subject is base-generated as the VP specifier, if each category has at most one specifier. It still is compatible with various versions of the "Subject in VP" hypothesis (Koopman and Sportiche 1988; Manzini 1988) according to which the thematic subject is adjoined to VP in a small clause configuration at D-structure. If floated quantifiers overtly manifest the basic position of the subject (Sportiche 1988a), the rigid order *tous beaucoup* in (i) provides evidence supporting this hypothesis, with the VP-adjoined subject position higher than the A′ specifier of VP.

(i) Ils ont tous beaucoup mangé
    'They have all a lot eaten'

The leftward-moved *tout/tous* of Kayne 1975 appears to occupy the Spec of VP position, as is shown by its incompatibility with *beaucoup* and by the fact that it follows *tous* "floated" from the subject:

(ii) Ils ont tous tout mangé
    'They have all everything eaten'

12. Notice that if the VP adjunction option is available, (30b) will have the following representation:

(i) Combien a-t-il [t [beaucoup résolu [t′ de problèmes]]]

t′ is not antecedent governed by t because of the intervening potential A′ binder *beaucoup*, which c-commands t′ but not t (according to our system of definitions).

The deviance of such examples as (30b) and (32b) is generally found less severe than the deviance of (31b). This is not surprising; the extraction from the indirect question involves an additional violation (perhaps of the Bounding Theory—consider the status of (31a)), and hence the cumulative effect can be expected to be stronger. Paradigms analogous to (31) have been occasionally noticed in other languages. For instance, Coopmans (1988) discusses a similar contrast determined by *wat voor* split in Dutch.

13. If the object moves to the object-agreement position and then *combien* alone is extracted, the resulting structure is ungrammatical:

(i) *Combien a-t-il [t de voitures] [conduites t]

In fact, the object-agreement position is not a Case position in French; there-fore, it cannot contain phonetically realized NP's at S-structure, owing to the Case Filter. As the amelioration induced by *en* extraction is only slight for many speakers (i.e., (34) remains quite marginal), there must be some inherent cost in the derivational option illustrated in (36) for reasons that we will not explore here. Obenauer's (1984, p. 173) proposal for the improved status of (34) is that here the whole object containing the trace of *en* is moved to Comp:

(ii) [combien t] il en a [beaucoup aimé t]
    'How many he of-them-has a lot loved'

But notice that extraction of *combien* with stranded *en* from a *wh* island remains strongly deviant:

(iii) *Combien ne sais-tu pas [comment en résoudre]

This is unexpected if the whole direct object can be extracted in such cases. I believe that representations like (ii) are ruled out for the reasons discussed in subsection 2.3.3 below.

14. Compare the corresponding French paradigm, in which the nonargumental nature of the equivalent of *as* is syntactically transparent:

(i) Pierre est ici, ce qu'ils savent / ne savent pas
    'Pierre is here, which they know / don't know'
(ii) Pierre est ici, comme ils le savent /*ne le savent pas
    'Pierre is here, as they know it / don't know it'

Here the clausal direct object is overtly pronominalized by *le*, and *comme* is a kind of manner adverbial ("Pierre is here, and things are the way in which they know them"). This suggests a similar analysis for the English construc-tion, perhaps with null complement anaphora of the clausal object.

15. For the sake of simplicity, we will continue to phrase our representations in terms of IP, I^0, etc. whenever the "split Infl" hypothesis is not crucial for the argument. An alternative possibility to the proposal in the text is that *pas* could fill the specifier position of an autonomous *neg* projection, present only in negative sentences (Pollock 1989; Moritz 1989).

Languages in which negation is represented by a clitic on the highest inflec-tional head (e.g. Italian) manifest identical Inner Island effects. I will assume that such clitics are A′ specifiers of some inflectional projection, or that they are moved at LF to a Spec position, or construed with a null operator in a Spec position, in the spirit of the analysis of affective elements to be proposed later in this section.

16. Many other problems, which will only be hinted at here, are left open. Subject-aux inversion can be triggered in embedded clauses in some cases:

(i) John said that in no case would he give up

This appears to require a (limited) recursion of CP's, perhaps along the lines of Chomsky 1977 (see Rizzi and Roberts 1989 for discussion). Inherently negative verbs seem to determine a weaker but detectable inner-island effect; compare the following:

(iii) How did he say that he fixed the car

(iv) How did he not say that he fixed the car

 (v) How did he deny that he fixed the car

Some speakers find (v) better than (iv) in the lower construal. This would be the immediate prediction of our system. If, on the other hand, the difference between (iv) and (v) is not significant, we are led to the conclusion that intrinsically negative verbs undergo movement in the syntax of LF, or that they are construed with a null negative operator. A similar approach would perhaps also account for the fact that modals in some cases appear to block embedded construals of preposed adjuncts (Travis 1984; D. Pesetsky, personal communication).

17. If an independent projection NegP is systematically available in negative sentences, and if this projection has an A' spec (Moritz 1989), an alternative possibility is that *no one* fills this position at LF. If the NegP is necessarily lower than the AgrP, the required lowering of *no one* in the syntax of LF could be analogous to the possible lowering of quantified NP's in raising constructions discussed in May 1977.

18. One cannot simply account for (65c) by stipulating that Affix Hopping requires adjacency because of Pollock's (1989, note 8) examples:

(i) a *John completely has lost his mind
     b   John has completely lost his mind
     c   John completely lost his mind

(ia) and (ib) show that *completely* cannot occur in pre-Infl position, but only between the highest inflectional head and the VP. But then in (ic) affix hopping must have taken place across the adverb; hence, it is not necessarily string-vacuous.

Negative adverbs such as *never* and *seldom*, which give rise to inner-island effects, apparently do not block Affix Hopping, contrary to negation:

(ii) a   John never arrived late
      b   John seldom arrived late
      c *John not arrived late

But notice that these elements can also appear in pre-Infl position contrary to *not*:

(iii) a   John never has arrived late
       b   John seldom has arrived late
       c *John not has arrived late

Therefore, (iiia) and (iiib) can have an LF representation in which the adverb does not intervene between the verbal trace and its A' antecedent; hence, no blocking effect is to be expected.

The alternation in (iv) cannot involve Affix Hopping of *to* across negation in the first case (Pollock 1989), as the resulting structure should be ruled out on a par with (65c).

(iv) a   He decided not to go
      b   He decided to not go

We must, rather, assume that *to* can be generated under T^0 (as in (iva)), and may optionally raise to Agr^0 (as in (ivb)), a case of regular head-to-head movement not affected by an intervening negation.

19. If a head can only be moved to another head, as per Chomsky's (1986b) generalized structure-preserving constraint, then perhaps the LF movement of the tensed verb forming the required A′-chain involves adjunction to Agr^0. Following Rizzi and Roberts 1989, I assume that all the familiar cases of syntactic head-to-head incorporation involve substitution, with adjunction possibly restricted to cliticization and, perhaps, to LF movement.

The order of elements in (65c) is possible in subjunctive clauses:

(i) I demand that he not smoke

Following Emonds 1976 and Roberts 1985, one can assume that a null subjunctive modal is involved in subjunctive clauses. This correctly predicts that movement of an auxiliary to C^0 will be blocked in such cases, under the Head Movement Constraint:

(ii) *I demand that under no circumstance be he arrested

(compare *I said that under no circumstance should he be arrested*). On the possibility of directly moving V^0 to C^0 in the Continental Scandinavian Languages, apparently skipping a null inflection, see Holmberg and Platzack 1988.

Chapter 2

1. One should further specify whether the choice of the canonical direction is unique in a grammatical system, and determined by the respective positions of verbs and objects, or whether the canonical direction can vary for different kinds of heads within the same language, and depends for each head on the position of the complement. On the former view, canonical government in German would be rigidly from right to left; on the latter view, canonical government in German would be from right to left for V^0 and I^0 and from left to right for C^0.

2. In Stowell's approach, Theta assignment involves coindexation with the appropriate slot of the Theta grid of the assigner. A Theta-marked object is then coindexed with (and in an extended sense bound by) the Theta-marking verb.

3. In a previous version of this chapter it was assumed, on the basis of the ill-formedness of VP preposing with exceptional Case Marking structures, that the VP of infinitival sentences is ungoverned:

(1) * . . . and [know the answer] I believe Bill to t

This assumption is clearly too strong, in view of the at least marginal acceptability of VP preposing with control infinitives. The question why (i) is significantly more degraded will be left open.

4. In French, sentences corresponding to (14a) are acceptable on a literary stylistic register. I agree with Deprez (1988) that this kind of inversion involves a *pro*, not a trace in subject position. On the licensing of nonreferential *pro* subject in French, see also Pollock 1986.

5. Chung and McCloskey (1987) point out that the rule of pronoun postposing in Irish can apply only when the pronoun is properly head-governed (by an inflectional head or by a higher predicate in small clauses). The similarity with Heavy NP Shift is striking, and the ECP provides a natural unified analysis.

6. We must assume here that a lexical head protects its specifier from external government. See the definitions in chapter 1, particularly in note 4.

7. This also has the desirable conclusion of excluding in principle a representation like (ii) for (i), while allowing (iii):

(i) Combien a-t-il conduit de voitures?

(ii) *[Combien t] a-t-il conduit t' de voitures

(iii) Combien a-t-il conduit [t de voitures]

(See note 9 of chapter 1.) It also implies that when *ne* is extracted from a direct object and *quanti* is *wh*-moved in Italian, the representation is (vi), not (v); hence, the specifier is extracted alone from the NP whose head has been cliticized:

(iv) Quanti ne hai visti?
'How many (you) of-them-have seen?'

(v) *[Quanti t] ne hai visti t'

(vi) Quanti ne hai visti [t' t]

We must then agree on this point with Kayne (1984, chapter 3), *contra* Belletti and Rizzi (1981).

8. How can the proper-government requirement be fulfilled on the trace of the moved auxiliary itself? Various possibilities come to mind. Perhaps the most natural is that the head-government requirement only holds for empty XP's as an independent requirement: for empty heads, head government is subsumed under antecedent government.

9. French also has a residual V-2 structure in main interrogatives (see Rizzi and Roberts 1989 and references quoted there), a relic of productive V-2 attested in previous stages of the language. By parity of reasoning, we would expect French not to allow the residual V-2 across a subject trace. Evidence supporting this conclusion is provided by Friedemann (1989), based on the distribution of interrogative *que*. This element, contrary to other *wh* elements in French, requires I-to-C movement (see (ib)); hence, it can never appear in embedded contexts, which exclude I-to-C movement (see (ic)).

(i) a Qu'as-tu dit t
'What have you said'
   b *Que tu as dit t
'What you have said'
   c *Je ne sais pas que tu as dit
'I don't know what you have said'
   d Qu'as-tu dit qui t est arrivé
'What did you say that happened'

e *Qu'est arrivé
   'What happened'

que can be moved from an object position, as in (ia), or from an embedded
subject position, as in (id), but not from a local subject position, as in (ie). If
I-to-C movement never licenses a subject trace in French, Friedemann argues,
the context required by *que* cannot be created in (ie); hence interrogative *que*
can never correspond to a local subject.

10. The generalization that emerges from the literature on German seems to
be the following: in the (southern) varieties of German in which object extraction is fully acceptable from a *dass* clause, subject extraction also is fully
acceptable (e.g., (38a) and (38b) are on a par and fully acceptable); in the
varieties in which object extraction is deviant to some extent, subject extraction is more severely ill-formed. This suggests (Fanselow 1987) that in the
restrictive dialects the spec of Comp of *dass* clauses cannot (easily) be used
for successive cyclic extraction of NP's. This determines a subjacency violation in the case of object extraction, and an additional violation of the head-
government requirement in the case of subject extraction (the head-government requirement is presumably fulfilled in the southern varieties through the
technique discussed in section 2.5). No comparable dialectal variation is found
in cases of subject extraction from embedded V-2 (see (36)), which is fully
acceptable in all varieties.

11. The contrast involving LF movement in the Bernese dialect reported in
note 15 also suggests that C^0 plays a crucial role in the licensing of a subject
trace in this OV language, as is assumed in the reference quoted.

12. The well-formedness of (35) and (36) also suggests that examples such as
(33a) should not be excluded via some version of the crossing constraint. (See
Pesetsky 1982b for relevant discussion.) A crossing analysis appears to be
unable to distinguish (33a) from the other cases.

13. In Italian and French, sentences like (43b) are fully natural and do not
require a particularly heavy subject.

(i) Con alla testa un grande scienziato, . . .
     'With at its head a great scientist, . . .'

This is surprising, as P in general does not license a trace in Romance languages. (i) might involve the licensing of an expletive *pro* (in which case the
construction would be assimilated to subject inversion), or it could be a case
of a small clause base-generated with the order predicate-subject (Contreras
1987), perhaps akin to the order found in the causative construction in
Romance languages (Manzini 1983).

14. We will leave open how the range of dialects allowing the *for-to* sequence
is to be treated. We will simply notice that the Belfast dialect discussed in
Borer 1989 and Henry 1989 allows the association of *for* with *to* as a complex
inflection, as is clearly shown by (i):

(i) I would prefer John for to go

We then expect *for* not to interfere with subject extraction in this dialect. Henry (1989) discusses this; her analysis in terms of a cliticization process attaching *for* to *to* recalls the case of the clitic complementizer in Hebrew (Shlonsky 1988) and the prepositional complementizers in Romance languages (Rizzi 1982a, chapter 3).

15. It should be noticed that the analysis of (48c) implies that traces created by LF movement must also be properly head-governed. This is not an uncontroversial assumption (see Aoun et al. 1987 for a different view); still, it permits an immediate account of ordinary superiority effects:

(i) *What did who do

(ii) *I wonder what who did

When *who* is moved in the syntax of LF, no proper head governor can be provided for it, as the Spec of C is already filled and the required agreement in C^0 (see section 2.5) cannot be triggered. As is predicted by this approach, LF movements of subjects and *why* seem to pattern on a par across languages. English and French disallow both, for the reasons just reviewed. According to Haider (1986), German allows both—possibly another consequence of the governing properties of C^0 capable of hosting the inflected verb. Chinese (Huang 1982) and Japanese (Lasnik and Saito 1984) also allow both, which means, in the terms of the current approach, that an appropriate head governor must be available (the identification of which will be left open here). Particularly clear evidence that traces created by LF movement require proper head government is provided by Bader and Penner (1988), who show that in the Bernese variety of Swiss German superiority violations, generally disallowed in embedded questions, become acceptable if C^0 is filled by the overt complementizer *dass*:

(iii) I frage mi [was [*(dass) [wär kchouft het]]]
     'I ask myself what that who bought has'

(This example is from page 32 of Bader and Penner 1988.) Their plausible interpretation is that the complementizer *dass* (an intrinsic governor in this dialect, as independent evidence shows) is necessary to fulfill the proper-government requirement on the subject trace after LF movement.

16. The fact that (51) is more severely ill-formed than (50c) can be understood if this kind of stylistic inversion involves a sort of chain composition at LF (absorption) between the inverted subject and the *wh* element akin to the one involved in multiple questions (Kayne 1984, 1986). The contrast between (51) and (50c) could then be related to the fact that *why* can much more easily allow multiple questions than *whether* or *if*. It should also be noticed that for some speakers (48c) is degraded with respect to the other examples, but not completely excluded; perhaps sentence adverbials can be very marginally attached to a lower position, from which movement is allowed.

17. If adjunct small clauses modifying the subject are base-generated within VP, as should be the case if subjects always start from the VP (see Roberts 1988a for arguments supporting this view), then this case may reduce to the case of adjunct small clauses predicated of objects, to be discussed below.

18. Ian Roberts notices that the object can bind an anaphor within an adjunct small clause (*I met Bill very angry at himself*), a property that is not expected in view of structure (58) and the standard assumption that the command relation relevant for the theory of Binding is strict c-command. Perhaps in a predication relation the "subject" is always allowed to bind an anaphor within its predicate, whether strict c-command holds or not (see Hellan's (1986) approach to long-distance binding); alternatively, one could assume that the AP always contains a null subject which is construed with the overt "subject of predication" and acts as the binder of an AP-internal anaphor. On the peculiar behavior of "reconstruction" with preposed AP's, which may support the latter view, see Barss 1986.

19. In Belletti and Rizzi 1988 it is argued that the experiencer of certain psychological verbs is base-generated as a daughter of VP at D-Structure:

(i) a NP [[worry this] John]
    b This [[worried t] John]

This hypothesis now raises a problem with respect to the proposed analysis, as the experiencer can be *wh*-moved:

(ii) Who did this worry?

Hence, the experiencer trace must be properly head-governed, which it should not be under the current assumptions. We must then revise the structure proposed in Belletti and Rizzi 1988 and assume that base-generated V′ recursion is possible, and that the experiencer is a daughter and sister of the V′ constituent in a kind of base-generated adjunction structure:

(iii)

Then the trace of *John* is governed by V within its immediate projection, V′, and all the other results permitted by structure (iii) (asymmetries in binding, Theta assignment, etc.) can be preserved.

20. That a moved inflected auxiliary is incompatible with a filled head of C is clearly shown in hypothetical clauses in English, where *if* and subject-aux inversion are complementary:

(i)   If John had done that, . . .

(ii) Had John done that, . . .

(iii) *If had John done that, . . .

As for I-to-C movement in the Germanic languages with preverbal V-2, we continue to assume that there the inflected verb is attracted by morphosyntactic features in C^0, which are morphologically subcategorized to host an inflected verb (see the approach to incorporation in Rizzi and Roberts 1989).

A C^0 endowed with such features is an intrinsic governor, a property which is not affected by the application of I-to-C movement.

21. The proposed approach excludes structures like (69) in a principled way if the language chooses Spec-head agreement in Comp as the device to allow subject extraction. If C^0 intrinsically possesses governing capacities and thus does not need agreement to become a proper head governor, then the equivalent of (69) should be allowed. This appears to be the case in Norwegian, as the following example from Hellan and Christensen 1986 shows:

(i) Petter vet jeg ikke [hva [t sa t]]
    'Peter know I not what said'

Engdahl (1985) conjectures that (i) is made possible by the inherent governing capacity of Comp in Norwegian, and explores other structural properties of the language which appear to correlate (subject parasitic gaps, possible extraction from left-branch constituents). See also Taraldsen 1986. On the apparently more limited intrinsic governing capacities of C^0 in the other Germanic languages, see section 2.3.5 and the references cited there.

22. On the fact that subject extraction cannot take place from postverbal position in Hebrew, see Shlonsky 1987, 1989. The English dialects allowing subject extraction across *that* may be amenable to the same analysis if they involve cliticization of *that*, as Anthony Kroch points out.

23. Also the linear definition would permit a principled explanation in this case, by relating the observed difference to the fact that French is SVO and West Flemish in SOV. This approach was adopted in Rizzi 1987.

24. Structures corresponding to (90b) are degraded if the verb is passivized:

(i) *?John, I was assured [t [t to be a nice guy]]

This suggests that the Case feature originates from the main verb, is then transmitted to C^0 under government, and is assigned under government and adjacency to the variable. (Adjacency then holds only on the actual assignment of case to a maximal projection, not on the transmission of a Case feature from head to head.) This analysis may be extendable to the following familiar contrast:

(ii) *I would prefer very much John to win

(iii) Who would you prefer very much to win?

(See Chomsky and Lasnik 1977 and Pesetsky 1982a.) A case feature could be transmitted from the main verb to Agr in Comp under government in (iii), and then assigned to the subject variable by Agr under government and adjacency. As (ii) involves no movement, and no intermediate governor in Comp can be licensed, assignment must take place directly from *prefer*, but the adjacency condition is not met. An extension of this analysis to *Who do you believe sincerely to VP* would require the nontrivial assumption that epistemic predicates can select untensed CP's (with agreement in Comp, which perhaps suffices to exclude PRO under the PRO Theorem).

25. Vata differs critically from Swedish in that a subject is never extractable from a *wh* island, whether or not its trace is spelled out (Koopman and Sportiche 1986, 1988). The analysis of this case will be left open here.

The economy guidelines should not have the effect of banning all sorts of optional processes, e.g., the *da die* rule in West Flemish. A theory of minimal effort in syntax thus seems to require a distinction between language-specific options resulting from particular fixations of parameters of UG (e.g., agreement in Comp) and marked language-specific rules (trace spellout, *do* insertion): only the latter should be blocked by the availability of a less costly device, while the former would remain fully optional. This necessary distinction is hard to make precise in general terms, but is relatively clear in some cases. For instance, various languages differ from Swedish and Vata in that they use resumptive pronouns as a matter of general parametric choice, not as specific rescuing devices for certain critical environments. In such cases the resumptive strategy can be freely used in structures in which the gap strategy would lead to a violation of the ECP or of some other principle, but we do not expect to find, in other environments, the same kind of strict complementarity that is manifested by trace spellout. This appears to be correct: for example, in headed relatives in Modern Hebrew the gap strategy and the resumptive strategy alternate freely in all the contexts in which specific principles do not block one strategy (Islands, ECP, Principle B, etc.; see Borer 1984). On the different properties of the resumptive strategy across languages, see Georgopoulos 1985, McCloskey and Sells 1989, Safir 1986, and Sells 1984. For a recent discussion see Tellier 1988.

26. The pattern manifested by Bani-Hassan, the Arabic dialect discussed in Kenstowicz 1984, suggests that the possibility of a principled approach should be considered with some caution. In this language, preverbal and postverbal subjects systematically differ in case making (*min* vs, *miin* (= who vs. whom) for the *wh* elements), and a subject extracted across an overt Comp always has the postverbal form (the following examples are from Kenstowicz 1984):

(i) Miin/*min Fariid gaal innu *pro* kisar t al-beeda?
    'Who   Fariid said that   broke the egg?'

But the dialect also allows the English strategy: the embedded C^0 can be null, and in that case the extracted subject obligatorily has the preverbal form:

(ii) Min/*miin Fariid gaal 0 t kisar al-beeda?
     'Who   Fariid said   broke the egg?'

In the terms developed in this chapter, the derivation of (ii) must involve movement of the subject from preverbal position to the Spec of Comp and agreement in Comp to license the subject trace. The fact that the English strategy and the Italian strategy apparently cannot be combined again recalls Chomsky's minimal-effort guidelines (a functional interpretation along similar lines is in fact proposed by Kenstowicz). The fact that movement from preverbal position is obviously possible in this Null Subject Language may suggest that the unavailability of short movement in other languages should not be given an account too tightly related to the positive setting of the Null Subject

Parameter. It should be noticed that there are other important differences between Italian and Bani-Hassan to which the observed difference could be related. One is that the unmarked word order with postverbal subjects is VOS in Italian and VSO in Bani-Hassan (Shlonsky 1987). A less conspicuous but possibly relevant difference is that Italian does not allow relative-clause extraposition from a preverbal subject (Rizzi 1984, chapter 1; Cardinaletti 1987), whereas Bani-Hassan does (I am grateful to Michael Kenstowicz for providing the relevant example):

(iii) *Un/l' uomo è arrivato ieri che ti conosce bene
      'A/the man arrived yesterday that knows you well

(iv) Al-zlima wisil alyoom alli 9arfak kwayyis
      'The man arrived yesterday that knows you well'

How the two distinct behaviors are to be properly expressed, and where the observed differences stem from, will be left open here.

27. In addition to the conceptual and formal inadequacies, a filtering approach to (109) would fail to distinguish this case from cases in which spec and head of Comp are both filled as a consequence of movement, as in main interrogatives:

(i) [what did [you t see t]]

From this perspective, languages allowing doubly filled Comps simply have a phonetically realized form for a +wh C^0 (which may or may not be identical to the overt −wh C^0; consider various Dutch, French and Italian dialects, Middle English, etc.). No variation in the form of Comp, in the number of positions available, etc. must be postulated in addition to this trivial lexical parameter. This seems to be a natural and minimal characterization of the parameter involved in the cross-linguistic variation on doubly filled Comp effects.

28. Independent evidence that an empty operator is intrinsically incompatible with agreement in Comp is possibly provided by the severe ill-formedness of structures involving subject parasitic gaps, such as the following:

(i) *The guy whom I met t [before [Op [t' left]]]

These structures are clearly more deviant than those manifesting the "surprising" asymmetries discussed in section 3.7. See Browning 1987 for a discussion. If the null operator involved in parasitic gaps (Chomsky 1986b) is intrinsically incompatible with agreement in Comp, the head-government requirement is violated by t' in (i).

29. This approach can be naturally extended to agreement in Comp with pseudo-relatives (*Je l'ai vu qui sortait du cinéma*); see Guasti 1988 and references cited there. Kayne (1984, chapter 3, note 23) notices that *that* cannot be omitted in relatives using the resumptive strategy in English:

(i) The book I got in the mail
(ii) The book *(that) I was wondering whether I would get it in the mail

This may now be interpretable along the following lines: a relative must be explicitly marked as predicated of the head; this explicit marking can be done by the overt or null operator when the movement strategy is used; when the resumptive strategy is used, the only available device is Comp agreement with the head; hence, the A-agreeing form of C^0 must be selected.

30. As subject relatives with a null C^0 appear to be possible in different varieties of English, it seems to be the case that these structures are not restricted to Null Subject Languages (Anthony Kroch, personal communication). It should be noticed that in our system nothing excludes the possibility— e.g., for a variety of English—of selecting a null form of C^0 manifesting A-agreement, which would make the relevant configuration possible. On the other hand, our analysis predicts that Null Subject languages should never manifest the kind of subject-object asymmetry in relatives that is attested in standard English.

Chapter 3

1. As is usual in current syntactic research, what is relevant is not the absolute acceptability of an example but its status relative to another example. The different diacritics are meant to express a relational judgment rather then absolute status.

2. (17d) is possible in the nonidiomatic interpretation of *credito* = financial credit. The same facts hold in French:

(i)   ?Quel privilège ne sais-tu pas à qui accorder?
(ii) *Quel crédit ne sais-tu pas à qui accorder?

(ii) is excluded in the relevant idiomatic interpretation.

3. In the same vein, Lasnik and Saito (1984, p. 268) notice the relatively mild ill-formedness of cases of subject extraction from a declarative embedded in a *wh* island (their numbers and diacritics):

(124) a   ?*Who do you wonder whether John said t came ?

They also notice that extraction of a subject deeply embedded within an island (in this case a Complex NP) tends to pattern with object extraction, not with adjunct extraction (actually, their choice of diacritics suggests fully parallel status for subjects and objects in this case):

(120) a   *Why do you believe the claim that John left t ?
      b   ?*What do you believe the claim that John bought t ?

(121) a   ?*Who do you believe the claim that John said t came ?

Lasnik and Saito also conclude that no ECP violation is involved in cases such as (121a) and (124a). See also the more detailed discussion in section 3.7 of the present monograph.

4. The necessity of a complete dissociation between subject and adjunct extraction is clearly indicated by the asymmetric behavior of extraction from a *wh* island in Norwegian, as was pointed out by Elisabet Engdahl. Subject extraction is fully acceptable, whereas adjunct extraction is excluded (Engdahl's examples):

(i) *Hvordan lurer du pa hvilket problem Jon vill lose?
     'How wonder you which problem John will solve?'
(ii) Hvem skjonner du ikke hva sier ?
     'Who understand you not what says?'

The case is distinct from the Italian case in that Norwegian is not a Null Subject language and does not allow free inversion; hence, structure (ii) cannot involve extraction from postverbal position. (ii) is well formed because the subject trace is properly head-governed by C^0, under Engdahl's (1985) analysis (see note 21 to chapter 2); (i) is ill formed, as the similar case in English, Italian, etc., because the required antecedent-government relation between the operator in the main Comp and its trace fails owing to Relativized Minimality. This analysis implies that the extractability of the subject is solely determined by the head-government requirement; no other condition must be met (in particular, antecedent government is not required), in spite of the fact that the subject is not theta-governed.

5. According to Aoun (1986), the nonreferential nature of adjunct traces has the property of not triggering the peculiar interplay of Principle A and Principle C that allows long-distance binding of ordinary referential variables in his system. According to Cinque's (1984) proposal, a nonreferential element cannot be the antecedent of a (resumptive) pronoun; hence, the use of a null resumptive pronoun, which underlies apparent island violations in Cinque's system, is not available with nonreferential adjuncts.

6. "Suppose that certain lexical items are designated as 'referential' and that by a general convention, each occurrence of a referential item is assigned a marker, say, an integer, as a feature. . . . The semantic component will then interpret two referential items as having the same reference just in case they are strictly identical—in particular, in case they have been assigned the same integer in the deep structure." (Chomsky 1965, pp. 145–146)

7. C-command and m-command (and, *a fortiori*, the elementary relations of precedence and dominance) can be looked at as the formal building blocks of the substantive relations of government and binding. Sisterhood, the fundamental structural relation exploited by Theta Theory, is too local to be used as a proper connecting device in the relevant sense, as it would never allow a connection to extend beyond the first dominating node.

8. This is a welcome result. According to Chomsky's (1986b) Bounding Theory, a subjacency barrier is a maximal projection that is not theta-governed. If postverbal subjects were theta-governed, one would expect extraction from a postverbal subject to be fully grammatical. In fact, this kind of extraction is slightly deviant (iii), and patterns by and large with extraction from a preverbal subject (ii), as opposed to the fully grammatical extraction from an object (i):

(i) Il libro di cui ho letto [il primo capitolo t]
     'The book of which I read the first chapter'
(ii) ?Il libro di cui [il primo capitolo t] mi ha convinto
     'The book of which the first chapter convinced me'

(iii) ?Il libro di cui mi ha convinto [il primo capitolo t]
'The book of which convinced me the first chapter'

(See Belletti and Rizzi 1988 for finer distinctions.) It seems appropriate to analyze (iii) as involving the crossing of at least one barrier, as is the case if the postverbal subject is not theta-governed, under the *Barriers* approach. This case also follows within Cinque's (forthcoming) approach, as the preverbal or postverbal subject is not selected by a head of the appropriate kind.

9. One might try to relate the slight asymmetry between locatives and temporals to the fact that, in Romance languages, locatives can be cliticized (*Mario ci ha comprato un libro*; 'Mario there-bought a book) whereas temporals cannot. Instrumentals can also be cliticized: *Mario ci ha aperto la porta*; 'Mario with-it-opened the door'). But locatives occurring with stative predicates cannot be cliticized and still allow extraction from indirect questions:

(i)   Mario è felice in questa città
      'Mario is happy in this town'

(ii) *Mario ci è felice
      'Mario there-is happy'

(iii) In quale città non sai se Mario sarebbe felice?
      'In what town do you wonder whether Mario would be happy?'

As for the apparent possibility of extracting a VP out of a *wh* island (see (8c) in chapter 2), we may think that an index on the VP is licensed by the event Theta role; alternatively, VP preposing might be akin to the case of adverbial PP preposing discussed in appendix 1 of the present chapter; see note 17.

10. Concerning examples like (37e), some speakers find extraction of an adjunct PP more acceptable than extraction of *why* (P. Coopmans, personal communication). Thus, for some speakers, (ii) in the relevant interpretation is somewhat less deviant than (i):

(i)   Why do you wonder whether he was fired t ?

(ii) For what reason do you wonder whether he was fired t ?

On our analysis, in principle the two traces could not be indexed, and the two examples should be equally deviant. This indeed is the judgment that many speakers give. But since other speakers appear to detect a distinction here, we should ask how it can arise. We can notice that the two examples differ in that theta-marking still takes place *within* the adjunct *wh* phrase in (ii), but not in (i) (no assigner and assignee can be distinguished within the one-word *wh* element). We can then suppose that (ii) allows for the marked possibility (not exploited by all speakers) of percolating the index of the NP up to the PP node (of which the NP is the "semantic head," in the sense of Abney 1987). This can marginally allow a binding connection to be established. No such marginal procedure can be available in the case of (i), there being no adjunct-internal theta-marking process. (i) is then more uniformly rejected. See also the last refinement of the present section based on Cinque 1989, for another factor which may differentiate (i) and (ii).

11. Alternatively, we could allow nonreferential elements to bear a different kind of indices, say superscripts, which would not enter into binding relations (restricted to referential indices) but which could be used in the definition of antecedent government. This device may also be appropriate to express agreement relations and dependencies in X^0 chains. The revision of definition (70) in appendix 2 of chapter 1 also is straightforward along the lines discussed in the text.

12. An A dependency connects an argument to a theta position in the typical case, but not always. In some structures the A dependency connects an expletive to an argument in a theta position:

(i) There seems t to be a horse in the garden

This sort of dependency also is strictly local, and disallows SuperRaising:

(ii) *There seems that it is likely t to be a horse in the garden

The account can be the same if we assume that (structural) case is a necessary ingredient for a chain to be visible at LF in the relevant sense (see chapter 6 of Chomsky 1981 and, for some refinements, Belletti 1988a). In (ii) the argument *a horse* should then form a chain with an element (necessarily a nonargument) bearing (structural) case. *It* does not qualify, as it it is not the appropriate expletive for nominal chains in English. *There* would qualify, but it is too far away to antecedent-govern t in (ii), and the required chain (*there*, t, *a horse*) cannot be formed.

The analysis proposed in the text extends to the class of cases of SuperRaising discussed by Lasnik (1985), illustrated by the following:

(iii) *John is believed (that) he likes t

t cannot form a proper chain with *he* (whether or not the two are coindexed) because the two positions are thematically independent, hence a Theta Criterion violation would arise; t cannot form a chain with *John* because the required antecedent government relation fails due to Relativized Minimality.

Notice that the incompatibility between a derived subject and an anaphoric clitic discussed in Rizzi 1986b still seems to require an independent stipulation of local binding in chain formation. The similarity between this chain condition and Relativized Minimality suggests that the former should ultimately be reduced to the latter, a topic which we will not address here.

13. Two more cases have been pointed out for Dutch by Koopman and Sportiche (1988). The first involves movement of the direct object. Koopman and Sportiche argue that extraction of the direct object from a *wh* island is significantly worse than extraction of a selected PP, but better than adjunct extraction. They analyze the case in a way consistent with the descriptive generalization summarized in (46); in fact, according to their analysis, direct objects (of the relevant kind) must be moved to the Spec of VP to receive case, and then adjoined to VP to circumvent a definiteness restriction. The latter trace appears to be the source of the deviance of the structure.

The second case is raised by the fact (Koopman and Sportiche 1988, note 39) that r-pronouns extracted from PP's via movement through the PP Spec (van Riemsdijk 1978) can be moved to the local Comp but cannot be extracted across a *wh* island.

14. In our system the presence of the trace in Comp is enforced for different reasons in (50a) and (50c). In (50a) it must be there to allow C^0 agreement, which provides a proper governor for the subject trace; in (50c) it must be there to establish a government connection (the only possible connection) between the operator and the variable. In (50b) the presence of the trace is fully optional—if it is there, its presence is licensed by the fact that it participates in establishing a government connection between the operator and the variable; if it is not there, chain formation is not possible, but the operator-variable connection is provided by binding. In (50a) and (50b) the connection is provided both by government and binding—a state of affairs that is not excluded by the system, which does not enforce uniqueness of connection. See below for evidence that a government connection is possible in cases like these.

15. Consider for instance the deviant extraction of direct objects in Dutch under the Koopman-Sportiche analysis (note 13 above). In this analysis, a direct object of the relevant kind must be moved to an A′ position adjoined to VP, owing to the interaction of Case requirements and other conditions. *Wh* movement then takes place from this position. If the trace in this position must be retained at LF (as is not implausible, since according to Koopman and Sportiche the passage through the VP adjoined position is required, among other things, in order to escape a definiteness effect), we are in a case comparable to long-distance subject extraction: the *wh* element and its variable can be connected through binding, no problem involving head government arises, but the intermediate trace in the VP adjoined position, not being part of a well-formed A′-chain, is not licensed at LF. We thus obtain the required gradation: extraction of a selected PP only determines a weak violation of bounding theory; adjunct extraction gives rise to the strongest violation, as the operator cannot be connected to its variable; and object extraction determines an intermediate violation, on a par with long subject extraction in English (the required connection can be established through binding, but the representation involves an illicit trace with respect of our interpretation of Chomsky's guidelines).

16. Other kinds of reconstruction do not need a chain of government relations. For instance, an anaphor contained with a *wh* phrase connected to its variable via binding across an island can still be properly interpreted:

(i) ?Which picture of himself do you wonder whether John likes ?

The contrast between scope reconstruction and reconstruction for Binding Principle A follows immediately from Cinque's approach, which can allow reconstruction to apply freely in all cases, and excludes scope reconstruction in cases like (54) owing to an intrinsic interpretive incompatibility. Another relevant consideration is that perhaps (i) does not involve reconstruction at all if principle A can be fulfilled at D-Structure, as in Belletti and Rizzi 1988.

17. Guglielmo Cinque points out that the analysis of adverbial PP preposing may naturally extend to the cases of VP preposing in English, which also (marginally) allows extraction from a *wh* island (see (8c) in chapter 2). In fact, there may be empirical evidence favoring this approach over the one mentioned in note 9. As was independently pointed out by Baltin (1989) and Roberts (1988, p. 119), when an adjectival predicate undergoing genuine *wh* movement is extracted from a *wh* island, the result has the status of an ECP violation, not of a mere Subjacency violation (examples (ii) and (iv) are taken from the references quoted):

(i)   How stupid do you think (that) Bill considers Pete t

(ii) *How stupid do you wonder whether Bill considers Pete t

(iii) How angry do you think that he became t

(iv) *How angry do you wonder whether he became t

If, in general, predicates were allowed to carry a referential index, the strong ill-formedness of (ii)–(iv) would be unexpected. It then appears more plausible to assume that predicates cannot carry referential indices—an assumption that is fully in the spirit of our approach to indices, and gives an immediate account of the status of (ii)–(iv). We are then led to assimilate simple VP preposing in English to adverbial PP preposing in Italian—two configurations that presumably do not involve an operator-variable structure, and as such do not trigger the relevant case of Relativized Minimality, given the extension suggested in this appendix. On the other hand (ii)–(iv), involving *wh* movement, clearly instantiate an operator-variable structure, and as such they invoke Relativized Minimality. Notice incidentally that the observed behavior of *wh* movement of predicates provides further evidence that the argument-adjunct distinction is not an accurate characterization of the relevant empirical generalization, as genuine adjuncts pattern with elements as diverse as lexically selected adverbials and measure phrases, idiomatic direct objects, specifiers of the direct object, and predicates. Again, the referential-nonreferential distinction appears to be closer to empirical adequacy.

18. The idea that a trace can be left in the specifier position of a NP is not unproblematic. First of all, such a trace should be governed from outside, but this is inconsistent with the assumption that a lexical head protects its specifier from external government (see note 4 to chapter 1), an assumption which has occasionally played a role in our argument. Though this conflict may be resolved by adopting some version of the DP hypothesis, at least one case of extraction from NP that we have discussed cannot be analyzed as involving a trace in Spec. This is the case of adnominal *en* extraction in French (subsection 2.3.3). As the NP containing the trace of *en* can be the (derived) subject, a trace in its Spec could not be properly head-governed. The question will be left open here.

19. A residual problem is the fact, observed by Chomsky (1986a), that nouns like *belief* cannot take a control complement in English, on a par with the corresponding verb:

(i) a *John believes [PRO to be immortal]
   b *The belief [PRO to be immortal] is widespread in this country

The extension of the standard account of (ia) to (ib) via the PRO Theorem would require PRO to be governed by the noun in (ib), contrary to what is predicted by the approach in the text. The plausibility of a structural explanation for this case is increased by the observation that in Italian, where the equivalent of (ia) is perfect, the equivalent of (ib) is quite acceptable, if somewhat marked:

(ii) a Gianni crede [di [PRO essere immortale]]
     'Gianni believes of to-be immortal'
   b La credenza [di [PRO essere immortali]] è molto diffusa in questo
     paese
     'The belief of to be immortal is very widespread in this country'

The property distinguishing (i) from (ii) is that in English S' Deletion (IP selection) appears to be compulsory, whereas in Italian a CP is selected in both cases, as indicated by the presence of the infinitival complementizer *di*. The question will be left open here. Borer's (1989) approach to the licensing and interpretation of control structures appears to be capable of drawing the necessary distinctions.

20. This approach makes a V+P reanalysis unnecessary for stranding, as the preposition alone in a stranding language suffices to satisfy the proper-head-government requirement. The descriptive generalization that unmarked stranding is possible only from argumental PP's in their basic position (Hornstein and Weinberg 1981) already follows from Huang's (1982) CED. The hypothesis of the necessity of a V+P reanalysis for stranding is seriously undermined by the relative well-formedness of parasitic gap structures such as (i) below (Kayne 1984, chapter 8), where the parasitic trace could not possibly be licensed via reanalysis with a verb.

(i) A man who close friends of t admire t

The contrast between NP movement (example (66)) and *wh* movement in (i) follows from the fact that NP movement requires a chain of antecedent-government relations for Theta-theoretic reasons—a chain which is blocked by the PP barrier. *Wh* movement does not require such a chain, because the operator-variable relation can be established via binding, a relation which is not affected by the intervention of the PP barrier.

References

Abney, S. 1987. The English Noun Phrase in its Sentential Aspect. PhD dissertation, MIT.

Acquaviva, P. 1989. Aspetti della complementazione frasale. Tesi di laurea, Università di Pisa.

Aoun, J. 1985. *A Grammar of Anaphora*. MIT Press.

Aoun, J. 1986. *Generalized Binding*. Foris.

Aoun, J., and R. Clark. 1985. "On Non-overt Operators." *Southern California Occasional Papers in Linguistics* 10: 17–36.

Aoun, J., and A. Li. 1989. "Scope and Constituency." *Linguistic Inquiry* 20: 141–172.

Aoun, J., and D. Sportiche. 1981. "On the Formal Theory of Government." *Linguistic Review* 2: 211–236.

Aoun, J., N. Hornstein, and D. Sportiche. 1981. "Aspects of Wide Scope Quantification." *Journal of Linguistic Research* 1: 67–95.

Aoun, J., N. Hornstein, D. Lightfoot, and A. Weinberg. 1987. "Two Types of Locality." *Linguistic Inquiry* 18: 537–577.

Bader, T., and Z. Penner. 1988. A Government-Binding Account of the Complementizer System in Bernese Swiss German. Arbeitspapier 25, Institut für Sprachwissenschaft, Universität Bern.

Baker, M. 1988. *Incorporation*. University of Chicago Press.

Baltin, M. 1989. "Comments on Cinque's paper 'The Respective Scope of Long and Successive Cyclic Movement.'" Paper presented at Second Princeton Workshop on Comparative Grammar, 1989.

Barss, A. 1986. Chains and Anaphoric Dependence. PhD dissertation, MIT.

Barwise, J., and R. Cooper. 1981. "Generalized Quantifiers and Natural Language." *Linguistics and Philosophy* 4: 159–219.

Bayer, J. 1984. "COMP in Bavarian." *Linguistic Review* 3: 209–274.

Bayer, J. 1989. Notes on the ECP in English and German. Manuscript, Max-Planck-Institut für Psycholinguistik, Nijmegen.

Belletti, A. 1988a. "The Case of Unaccusatives." *Linguistic Inquiry* 19: 1–34.

Belletti, A. 1988b. Generalized Verb Movement: On Some Differences and Similarities between Italian and French. Talk presented at GLOW Conference, Budapest.

Belletti, A. 1989. Agreement and Case in Past Participial Clauses in Italian. Manuscript, Scuola Normale Superiore di Pisa, Université de Genève.

Belletti, A., and L. Rizzi. 1981. "The Syntax of *ne*: Some Theoretical Implications." *Linguistic Review* 1: 117–154.

Belletti, A., and L. Rizzi. 1988. "Psych-Verbs and Theta Theory." *Natural Language and Linguistic Theory* 6, no. 3: 291–352.

Bennis, H., and L. Haegeman. 1984. "On the Status of Agreement and Relative Clauses in West Flemish." In *Sentential Complementation*, ed. W. de Geest and Y. Putseys (Foris).

Borer, H. 1984. "Restrictive Relatives in Modern Hebrew." *Natural Language and Linguistic Theory* 2: 219–260.

Borer, H. 1989. "Anaphoric Agr." In *The Null Subject Parameter*, ed. O. Jaeggli and K. Safir (Kluwer).

Brandi, L., and P. Cordin. 1981. "Dialetti e italiano: un confronto sul parametro del soggetto nullo." *Rivista di grammatica generativa* 6: 33–87.

Brandi, L., and P. Cordin. 1989. "Two Italian Dialects and the Null Subject Parameter." In *The Null Subject Parameter*, ed. O. Jaeggli and K. Safir (Kluwer).

Bromberger, S. 1986. What We Don't Know When We Don't Know Why. Manuscript, MIT.

Browning, M. 1987. Null Operator Constructions. PhD dissertation, MIT.

Browning, M. 1989. Comments on *Relativized Minimality*. Paper presented at Second Princeton Workshop on Comparative Grammar.

Burzio, L. 1986. *Italian Syntax*. Reidel.

Burzio, L. 1989. The Role of the Antecedent in Anaphoric Relations. Manuscript, Harvard University.

Cardinaletti, A. 1987. "Aspetti sintattici dell'estraposizione della frase relativa." *Rivista di grammatica generativa* 12: 3–59.

Carstens, V., and Kinyalolo. 1989. Agr, Tense, Aspect and the IP Structure: Evidence from Bantu. Paper presented at GLOW Conference, Utrecht.

Chomsky, N. 1957. *Syntactic Structures*. Mouton.

Chomsky, N. 1965. *Aspects of the Theory of Syntax*. MIT Press.

Chomsky, N. 1977. "On Wh Movememt." In *Formal syntax*, ed. P. Culicover, T. Wasow, and A. Akmajian (Academic).

Chomsky, N. 1981. *Lectures on Government and Binding*. Foris.

Chomsky, N. 1982. *Some Concepts and Consequences of the Theory of Government and Binding*. MIT Press.

Chomsky, N. 1986a. *Knowledge of Language*. Praeger.

Chomsky, N. 1986b. *Barriers*. MIT Press.

Chomsky, N. 1988. Some Notes on the Economy of Derivations and Representations. Manuscript, MIT.

Chomsky, N., and H. Lasnik. 1977. "Filters and Control." *Linguistic Inquiry* 8: 425–504.

Chung, S., and J. McCloskey. 1987. "Government, Barriers and Small Clauses in Modern Irish." *Linguistic Inquiry* 18: 173–237.

Cinque, G. 1980. "Extraction from NP in Italian." *Journal of Italian Linguistics* 5, no. 1: 47–99.

Cinque, G. 1984. A-bar Bound *pro* vs. Variable. Manuscript, University of Venice.

Cinque, G. 1989. On the Scope of 'Long' and 'Successive' Cyclic Movement. Paper presented at Second Princeton Workshop on Comparative Grammar.

Cinque, G. *Types of A' Dependencies*. MIT Press, forthcoming.

Contreras, H. 1986. Chain Theory, Parasitic Gaps, and the ECP. Manuscript, University of Washington, Seattle.

Contreras, H. 1987. "Small Clauses in Spanish and English." *Natural Language and Linguistic Theory* 5, no. 2: 225–244.

Coopmans, P. 1988. "On Extraction from Adjuncts in VP." In *Proceedings of WCCFL 1988*.

Couquaux, D. 1979. "Sur la syntaxe des phrases prédicatives en français." *Linguisticae Investigationes* 3: 245–284.

Culicover, P., and M. Rochemont. 1987. Stylistic Constructions and the Theory of Grammar. Manuscript, University of Arizona and University of British Columbia.

de Cornulier, B. 1974. "'Pourquoi' et l'inversion du sujet non clitique." In Actes du colloque franco-allemand de grammaire transformationnelle, ed. C. Rohrer and N. Ruwet (Niemeyer).

den Besten, H. 1983. "On the Interaction of Root Transformations and Lexical Deletive Rules." In *On the Formal Syntax of Westgermania*, ed. W. Abraham (Benjamins).

Deprez, V. 1988. Stylistic Inversion and Verb Movement. Manuscript, MIT.

Dobrovie-Sorin, C. 1990. "Clitic Doubling, *Wh* Movement, and Quantification in Romanian." *Linguistic Inquiry* 21, no. 3.

Doron, E. 1983. Verbless Predicates in Hebrew. PhD dissertation, University of Texas, Austin.

Emonds, J. 1976. *A Transformational Approach to English Syntax*. Academic.

Emonds, J. 1978. "The Verbal Complex V'-V in French." *Linguistic Inquiry* 9: 151–175.

Engdahl, E. 1985. "Parasitic Gaps, Resumptive Pronouns, and Subject Extractions." *Linguistics* 23: 3–44.

Fanselow, G. 1987. *Konfigurationalität*. Gunter Narr Verlag.

Frampton, J. 1989. "Parasitic Gaps and the Theory of Wh Chains." *Linguistic Inquiry* 21, no. 1: 49–77.

Friedemann, M.-A. 1989. Le pronom interrogatif *que*. Manuscript, Université de Genève.

Georgopoulos, C. 1985. "Variables in Palauan Syntax." *Natural Language and Linguistic Theory* 3: 59–94.

Giorgi, A. 1985. "The Proper Notion of C-command and the Binding Theory: Evidence from NP." *NELS* 16: 169–185.

Giorgi, A., and G. Longobardi. 1987. The Syntax of NP's: Configuration, Parameter and Empty Categories. Manuscript, Venice and Povo.

Giusti, G. 1988. Zu-infinitivals and the Structure of IP in German. Manuscript, University of Venice.

Godard, D. 1985. Propositions relatives, relations anaphoriques et prédication. Thèse d'Etat, Université de Paris 7.

Grimshaw, J. 1975. "Evidence for Relativization by Deletion in Chaucerian Middle English." In *Papers in the History and Structure of English*, ed. J. Grimshaw. (University of Massachusetts Occasional Papers, no. 1).

Grimshaw, J. 1979. "Complement Selection and the Lexicon." *Linguistic Inquiry* 10: 279–326.

Guasti, M. T. 1988. "La pseudorelative et les phénomènes d'accord." *Rivista di grammatica generative* 13: 35–57.

Haegeman, L. 1983. "*Die* and *dat* in West-Flemish Relative Clauses." In *Linguistics in the Netherlands*, ed. H. Bennis and W. U. S. van Lessen-Kloeke (Foris).

Haegeman, L. *Generative Syntax: Theory and Description—A Case Study from West Flemish*. Cambridge University Press, forthcoming.

Haider, H. 1986. "Affect α: A Reply to Lasnik and Saito, 'On the Nature of Proper Government.'" *Linguistic Inquiry* 17: 113–126.

Haider, H., and M. Prinzhorn, eds. 1986. *Verb Second Phenomena in Germanic Languages*. Foris.

Hellan, L. 1986. "On Anaphora and Predication in Norwegian." In *Topics in Scandinavian Syntax*, ed. Hellan and Christensen (Kluwer).

Hellan, L., and K. Koch Christensen, eds., 1986. *Topics in Scandinavian Syntax*. Kluwer.

Henry, A. 1989. Infinitives in a *for-to* Dialect. Manuscript, University of Ulster at Jordanstown and MIT.

Higginbotham, J. 1985. "On Semantics." *Linguistic Inquiry* 16: 547–593.

Hoekstra, T. 1984. "Government and the Distribution of Sentential Complementation in Dutch." In *Sentential Complementation*, ed. W. de Geest and Y. Putseys (Foris).

Holmberg, A., and C. Platzack. 1988. "On the Role of Inflection in Scandinavian Syntax." *Working Papers in Scandinavian Syntax* 42: 25–43.

Hornstein, N., and A. Weinberg. 1981. "Case Theory and Preposition Standing." *Linguistic Inquiry* 12: 55–92.

Huang, J. 1982. Logical Relations in Chinese and the Theory of Grammar. PhD dissertation, MIT.

Jaeggli, O. 1982. *Topics in Romance Syntax*. Foris.

Jaeggli, O. 1984. "Subject Extraction and the Null Subject Parameter." NELS 14: 132–153.

Jaeggli, O. 1985. On Certain ECP Effects in Spanish. Manuscript, USC.

Jaeggli, O., and K. Safir, eds. 1989. *The Null Subject Parameter*. Kluwer.

Kayne, R. 1974. "French Relative *que*." *Recherches linguistiques* 2–3: 27–92.

Kayne, R. 1975. *French Syntax*. MIT Press.

Kayne, R. 1984. *Connectedness and Binary Branching*. Foris.

Kayne, R. 1985. "L'accord du participe passé en français et en italien." *Modèles linquistiques* 7, no. 1: 73–89.

Kayne, R. 1986. "Connexité et inversion du sujet." In *La grammaire modulaire*, ed. M. Ronat and D. Couquaux (Editions de Minuit).

Kayne, R. 1989. "Null Subjects and Clitic Climbing." In *The Null Subject Parameter*, ed. O. Jaeggli and K. Safir (Kluwer).

Kayne, R., and J.-Y. Pollock. 1978. "Stylistic Inversion, Successive Cyclicity, and Move NP in French." *Linguistic Inquiry* 9: 595–621.

Kenstowicz, M. 1984. "The Null Subject Parameter in Modern Arabic Dialects." NELS 14: 207–219.

Keyser, S. J. 1975. "A Partial History of the Relative Clause in English." In *Papers in the History and Structure of English*, ed. J. Grimshaw (University of Massachusetts Occasional Papers, no. 1).

Kiparsky, C., and P. Kiparsky. 1971. "Fact." In *Semantics*, ed. D. Steinberg and L. Jakobovits (Cambridge University Press).

Klima, E. 1964. "Negation in English." In *The Structure of Language*, ed. J. Katz and J. Fodor (Prentice-Hall).

Koopman, H. 1983. "ECP Effects in Main Clauses." *Linguistic Inquiry* 14: 346–351.

Koopman, H. 1984. *The Syntax of Verbs*. Foris.

Koopman, H., and D. Sportiche. 1986. "A Note on Long Extraction in Vata and the ECP." *Natural Language and Linguistic Theory* 4: 367–374.

Koopman, H., and D. Sportiche. 1988. Subjects. Manuscript, UCLA.

Koster, J. 1984. "On Binding and Control." *Linguistic Inquiry* 15: 417–459.

Koster, J. 1987. *Domains and Dynasties*. Foris.

Ladusaw, W. 1981. "On the Notion *Affective* in the Analysis of Negative Polarity Items." *Journal of Linguistic Research* 1: 1–16.

Lasnik, H. 1981. "Restricting the Theory of Transformations: A Case Study." In *Explanation in Linguistics*, ed. N. Hornstein and D. Lightfoot (Longman).

Lasnik, H. 1985. "A Note on Illicit NP Movement." *Linguistic Inquiry* 16: 481–490.

Lasnik, H., and M. Saito. 1984. "On the Nature of Proper Government." *Linguistic Inquiry* 15: 235–289.

Liberman, M. 1974. "On Conditioning the Rule of Subject Aux Inversion." NELS 5: 77–91.

Lobeck, A. 1986. "VP Ellipsis in Infinitives: INFL as a Proper Governor." NELS 17: 425–442.

Longobardi, G. 1984. L'estrazione dalle 'isole' e lo *scope* dei sintagmi quantificati. Manuscript, Scuola Normale Superiore, Pisa.

Longobardi, G. 1985. "Connectedness, Scope and C-command." *Linguistic Inquiry* 16: 163–192.

Longobardi, G. 1987. "Extraction from NP and the Proper Notion of Head Government." In Giorgi and Longobardi 1987.

Longobardi, G. (forthcoming) Movement, Scope and Island Constraints. Manuscript, University of Venice.

Maling, J., and A. Zaenen. 1978. "The Nonuniversality of Surface Filters." *Linguistic Inquiry* 9: 475–497.

Manzini, M. R. 1983. Restructuring and Reanalysis. PhD dissertation, MIT.

Manzini, M. R. 1988. "Constituent Structure and Locality." In *Constituent Structure*, ed. A. Cardinaletti, G. Cinque, and G. Giusti (Foris).

Marantz, A. 1984. *On the Nature of Grammatical Relations*. MIT Press.

Marchini, L. 1986. "Le interrogative W nella lingua tedesca." *Rivista di grammatica generativa* 11: 99–125.

May, R. 1977. The Grammar of Quantification. PhD dissertation, MIT.

May, R. 1985. *Logical Form: Its Structure and Derivation*. MIT Press.

McCloskey, J., and P. Sells. 1989. "Resumptive Pronouns, A' Binding and Levels of Representation in Irish." In *The Syntax of Modern Celtic Languages, Syntax and Semantics*, ed. R. Henrick (Academic).

Milner, J.-C. 1978. *De la syntaxe à l'interprétation*. Seuil.

Milner, J.-C. 1982. *Ordres et raisons de langue*. Seuil.

Moritz, L. 1989. Syntaxe de la négation de phrase en français et en anglais. Mémoire de licence, Université de Genève.

Moro, A. 1988. "Per una teoria unificata della frasi copulari." *Rivista di grammatica generativa* 13: 81–110.

Motapanyane, V. 1988. La position du sujet dans une langue à l'ordre SVO/VSO. Mémoire de pré-doctorat, Université de Genève. *Rivista di grammatica generativa* 14: 75–103.

Obenauer. H. 1976. *Etudes de syntaxe interrogative du français*. Niemeyer.

Obenauer, H. 1984. "On the Identification of Empty Categories." *Linguistic Review* 4, no. 2: 153–202.

Obenauer, H. (forthcoming) *Aspects de la syntaxe A'*. Thèse d'Etat, Université de Paris 8.

Perlmutter, D. 1971. *Deep and Surface Structure Constraints in Syntax*. Holt, Rinehart & Winston.

Pesetsky, D. 1982a. "Complementizer-trace Phenomena and the Nominative Island Condition." *Linquistic Review* 1: 297–343.

Pesetsky, D. 1982b. Paths and Categories. PhD dissertation, MIT.

Pesetsky, D. 1984. "Extraction Domains and a Surprising Subject/Object Asymmetry." *GLOW Newsletter* 12: 58–60.

Pesetsky, D. 1987. "Wh in situ: Movement and Unselective Binding." In *The Representation of (In)definiteness*, ed. E. Reuland and A. ter Meulen (MIT Press).

Pollock, J.-Y. 1986. "Sur la syntaxe de 'en' et le paramètre du sujet nul." In *La grammaire modulaire*, ed. D. Couquaux and M. Ronat (Minuit).

Pollock, J.-Y. 1988. Extraction from NP in French and English: A Case Study in Comparative Syntax. Manuscript, Université de Rennes 2.

Pollock, J.-Y. 1989. "Verb Movement, UG and the Structure of IP." *Linguistic Inquiry* 20: 365–424.

Postal, P. 1974. *On Raising*. MIT Press.

Raposo, E. 1988. "Romance Inversion, the Minimality Condition, and the ECP." *NELS* 18: 357–374.

Reinhart, T. 1976. The Syntactic Domain of Anaphora. PhD dissertation, MIT.

Reuland, E. 1983. "Governing -ing." *Linguistic Inquiry* 14: 101–136.

Rizzi, L. 1982a. *Issue in Italian Syntax*. Foris.

Rizzi, L. 1982b. "Comments on Chomsky's Chapter 'On The Representation of Form and Function.'" In *Perspectives on Mental Representation*, ed. J. Mehler, E. Walker, and M. Garrett (Erlbaum).

Rizzi, L. 1984. *Spiegazione e teoria grammaticale*. CLESP, Padua (second printing: Unipress, Padua, 1990).

Rizzi, L. 1986a. "Null Objects in Italian and the Theory of *pro*." *Linguistic Inquiry* 17: 501–557.

Rizzi, L. 1986b. "On Chain Formation." In *The Grammar of Pronominal Clitics—Syntax and Semantics, Volume 19*, ed. H. Borer (Academic).

Rizzi, L. 1987. Relativized Minimality. Manuscript, Stanford University and Université de Genève.

Rizzi, L. 1988. On the Status of Referential Indices in Syntax. Paper presented at "The Chomskian Turn," Tel-Aviv and Jerusalem.

Rizzi, L. 1989. "On the Anaphor-Agreement Effect." *Rivista di linguistica*.

Rizzi, L., and I. Roberts. 1989. "Complex Inversion in French." *Probus* 1, no. 1: 1–30.

Roberts, I. 1985. "Agreement Parameters and the Development of English Modal Auxiliaries." *Natural Language and Linguistic Theory* 3: 21–58.

Roberts, I. 1988a. "Predicative AP's." *Linguistic Inquiry* 19: 703–710.

Roberts, I. 1988b. "Thematic Interveners." *Rivista di grammatica generativa* 13: 111–136.

Ross, J. R. 1983. Inner Islands. Manuscript, MIT.

Ruwet, N. 1972. *Théorie syntaxique et syntaxe du français*. Seuil.

Ruwet, N. 1982. *Grammaire des insultes et autres études*. Seuil.

Safir, K. 1985. *Syntactic Chains*. Cambridge University Press.

Safir, K. 1986. "Relative Clauses in a Theory of Binding and Levels." *Linguistic Inquiry* 17: 663–689.

Saito, M. 1984. "On the Definition of C-command and Government." *NELS* 14: 402–417.

Schneider-Zioga, P. 1987. Syntax Screening. Paper, USC, Los Angeles.

Schwartz, B., and S. Vikner. 1989. "All V-2 Clauses are CP's." *Working Papers in Scandinavian Syntax* 43: 27–50.

Scorretti, M. 1981. "Complementizer Ellipsis in 15th Century Italian." *Journal of Italian Linguistics* 6, no. 1: 35–46.

Sells, P. 1984. Syntax and Semantics of Resumptive Pronouns. PhD dissertation, GLSA, University of Massachusetts, Amherst.

Shlonsky, U. 1987. Null and Displaced Subjects. PhD dissertation, MIT.

Shlonsky, U. 1988. "Complementizer-cliticization in Hebrew and the ECP." *Natural Language and Linguistic Theory* 6, no. 2: 191–206.

Siloni, T. 1989. La semi-relative, l'état construit et l'analyse DP. Séminaire de recherche, Université de Genève.

Sobin, N. 1987. "The Variable Status of Comp-Trace Phenomena."*Natural Language and Linguistic Theory* 5, no. 1: 33–60.

Sportiche, D. 1988a. "A Theory of Floating Quantifiers and its Corollaries for Constituent Structure." *Linguistic Inquiry* 19: 425–449.

Sportiche, D. 1988b. Conditions on Silent Categories. Manuscript, UCLA.

Stowell, T. 1981. Origins of Phrase Structure. PhD dissertation, MIT.

Stowell, T. 1985. Null Operators and the Theory of Proper Government. Manuscript, UCLA.

Stowell, T. 1986. "Null Antecedents and Proper Government." *NELS* 16: 476–492.

Szabolcsi, A. 1987. "Functional Categories in the Noun Phrase." In *Approaches to Hungarian*, volume 2, ed. I. Kenesei (University of Budapest).

Taraldsen, K. T. 1986. "*Som* and the Binding Theory." In *Topics in Scandinavian Syntax*, ed. L. Hellan and K. Koch Christensen (Kluwer).

Tellier, C. 1988. Universal Licensing: Implications for Parasitic Gap Constuctions. PhD dissertation, McGill University.

Thiersch, C. 1978. Topics in German Syntax. PhD dissertation, MIT.

Tomaselli, A. 1989. La sintassi del verbo finito nelle lingue germaniche. Tesi di dottorato, Università di Pavia.

Torrego, E. 1985. On Empty Categories in Nominals. Manuscript, University of Massachusetts, Boston.

Travis, L. 1984. Parameters and Effects of Word Order Variation. PhD dissertation, MIT.

van Riemsdijk, H. 1978. *A Case Study in Syntactic Markedness*. Foris.

van Riemsdijk, H. 1989. Swiss Relatives. Paper presented at Second Princeton Workshop in Comparative Syntax.

Wanner, D. 1981. "Surface Complementizer Deletion: Italian *che- 0.*" *Journal of Italian Linguistics* 6, no. 1: 47–82.

Williams, E. 1987. "NP Trace in Theta Theory." *Linguistics and Philosophy* 10: 433–447.

Williams, E. 1986. "A Reassignment of the Functions of LF," *Linguistic Inquiry* 17: 265–299.

Zagona, K. 1988. *Verb Phrase Syntax*. Kluwer.

Index